Students' Rights

Other books in the Issues on Trial series:

Civil Liberties and War
The Environment
Reproductive Rights

Students' Rights

Laura K. Egendorf, Book Editor

GREENHAVEN PRESS
An imprint of Thomson Gale, a part of The Thomson Corporation

Detroit • New York • San Francisco • San Diego • New Haven, Conn.
Waterville, Maine • London • Munich

LIBRARY OF CONGRESS CATALOGING-IN-PUBLICATION DATA

Students' rights / Laura K. Egendorf, book editor.
    p. cm. -- (Issues on Trial)
Includes bibliographical references and index.
ISBN 0-7377-2509-5 (lib. : alk. paper)
    1. Students--Civil rights--United States. 2. Students--Legal status, laws, etc.--United States. I. Egendorf, Laura K., 1973– II. Series.
    KF4150.S778 2006
    344.73'079--dc22
                                                            2005052690

Printed in the United States of America
10 9 8 7 6 5 4 3 2 1

Contents

Chapter 1: The Right of Schools to Search Students

surveillance and lack virtually all rights to privacy or freedom from searches.

Chapter 2: Limiting Students' Right to Free Expression

A law professor asserts that high school newspapers are not equivalent to professional media and therefore are not entitled to the same First Amendment protections.

Chapter 3: Permitting Drug Tests for Student Athletes

Chapter 4: The Pledge of Allegiance and the First Amendment

An Internet columnist asserts that the Pledge of Allegiance is not a method of religious coercion and that the Supreme Court must declare it constitutional.

A pastor maintains that the Pledge of Allegiance is offensive because it indoctrinates students into worshipping their government at the expense of their personal freedoms.

Foreword

The U.S. courts have long served as a battleground for the most highly charged and contentious issues of the time. Divisive matters are often brought into the legal system by activists who feel strongly for their cause and demand an official resolution. Indeed, subjects that give rise to intense emotions or involve closely held religious or moral beliefs lay at the heart of the most polemical court rulings in history. One such case was *Brown v. Board of Education* (1954), which ended racial segregation in schools. Prior to *Brown*, the courts had held that blacks could be forced to use separate facilities as long as these facilities were equal to that of whites.

For years many groups had opposed segregation based on religious, moral, and legal grounds. Educators produced heartfelt testimony that segregated schooling greatly disadvantaged black children. They noted that in comparison to whites, blacks received a substandard education in deplorable conditions. Religious leaders such as Martin Luther King Jr. preached that the harsh treatment of blacks was immoral and unjust. Many involved in civil rights law, such as Thurgood Marshall, called for equal protection of all people under the law, as their study of the Constitution had indicated that segregation was illegal and un-American. Whatever their motivation for ending the practice, and despite the threats they received from segregationists, these ardent activists remained unwavering in their cause.

Those fighting against the integration of schools were mainly white southerners who did not believe that whites and blacks should intermingle. Blacks were subordinate to whites, they maintained, and society had to resist any attempt to break down strict color lines. Some white southerners charged that segregated schooling was *not* hindering blacks' education. For example, Virginia attorney general J. Lindsay Almond asserted, "With the help and the sympathy and the love and respect of the white people of the South, the colored man has risen under that educational process to a place of eminence and respect throughout the nation. It has served him well." So when the Supreme Court ruled against the segregationists in *Brown*, the South responded with vociferous cries of protest. Even government leaders criticized the decision. The governor of Arkansas, Orval Faubus, stated that he would not "be a party to any attempt to force acceptance of change to which the people are so overwhelmingly opposed." Indeed, resistance to integration was so great that when black students arrived at the formerly all-white Central High School in Arkansas, federal troops had to be dispatched to quell a threatening mob of protesters.

Nevertheless, the *Brown* decision was enforced and the South integrated its schools. In this instance, the Court, while not settling the issue to everyone's satisfaction, functioned as an instrument of progress by forcing a major social change. Historian David Halberstam observes that the *Brown* ruling "deprived segregationist practices of their moral legitimacy. . . . It was therefore perhaps the single most important moment of the decade, the moment that separated the old order from the new and helped create the tumultuous era just arriving." Considered one of the most important victories for civil rights, *Brown* paved the way for challenges to racial segregation in many areas, including on public buses and in restaurants.

In examining *Brown*, it becomes apparent that the courts play an influential role—and face an arduous challenge—in shaping the debate over emotionally charged social issues. Judges must balance competing interests, keeping in mind the high stakes and intense emotions on both sides. As exemplified by *Brown*, judicial decisions often upset the status quo and initiate significant changes in society. Greenhaven Press's Issues on Trial series captures the controversy surrounding influential court rulings and explores the social ramifications of such decisions from varying perspectives. Each anthology highlights one social issue—such as the death penalty, students' rights, or wartime civil liberties. Each volume then focuses on key historical and contemporary court cases that helped mold the issue as we know it today. The books include a compendium of primary sources—court rulings, dissents, and immediate reactions to the rulings—as well as secondary sources from experts in the field, people involved in the cases, legal analysts, and other commentators opining on the implications and legacy of the chosen cases. An annotated table of contents, an in-depth introduction, and prefaces that overview each case all provide context as readers delve into the topic at hand. To help students fully probe the subject, each volume contains book and periodical bibliographies, a comprehensive index, and a list of organizations to contact. With these features, the Issues on Trial series offers a well-rounded perspective on the courts' role in framing society's thorniest, most impassioned debates.

Introduction

While they may think of themselves as young adults, teen-agers—particularly if they are not yet eighteen years old—do not have the same level of constitutional rights as their parents or legal guardians. If they swear or speak disrespectfully to their parents, they may find their right to free speech restricted. Parents concerned about their child's activities may search through bedrooms and personal belongings without fear of violating the Fourth Amendment.

When they leave home in the morning and head to school, the rights of teenagers do not expand. This is because schools have long been understood to fill the parental role, a right known as in loco parentis. The term, which literally means "in the place of the parent," essentially places teenagers under two guardians—their parents and their school administrators. The idea of in loco parentis was originally established by eighteenth-century British legal scholar William Blackstone, who wrote that a father of school-age children "may . . . delegate part of his parental authority, during his life to the tutor or schoolmaster of the child; who is then in loco parentis, and has such a portion of the power of the parents committed to his charge." Professor of education Anthony E. Conte explains in an article for *Education*, "The doctrine of in loco parentis was imported from English law as a responsibility and protection for American teachers who felt the need to administer corporal punishment to students. From the outset of public education in the United States, educators have served as parents or guardians."

However, as its political tenor has changed over the years, the U.S. Supreme Court has often reinterpreted the doctrine. Schools began to lose their ability to control the behavior of students in the 1960s and 1970s, when the court was fairly liberal. During the 1980s, as the Supreme Court became more conservative, a number of decisions swung the pendulum back in favor of the schools, a situation that continues into the twenty-first century. Some commentators have lauded the expansion of school powers. For example, John C. Hogan writes in *The Schools, the Courts, and the Public Interest*, "Many of the benefits of parental authority are missing in the home. ... Under these circumstances, the school authorities, acting in loco parentis, must perform a very great public service that extends beyond the traditional bounds of public education." Other observers maintain that these rights go too far and that the powers granted to schools undermine parental authority.

The 1960s and 1970s were an era of Supreme Court decisions that expanded constitutional rights, such as *Miranda v. Arizona* and *Roe v. Wade*, and the justices' views on students' rights followed suit. In 1969, in *Tinker v. Des Moines School District*, the Supreme Court declared that students can speak out on political issues on school grounds as long as their speech is not disruptive. The lower courts followed with similar rulings; for example, the U.S. Court of Appeals for the Fourth Circuit ruled in *Quarterman v. Byrd* (1971) that schools could not forbid students from distributing an "underground" newspaper on campus. However, since the mid-1980s, the rights of students have steadily decreased as schools have been given greater authority. Among the cases that have curtailed students' rights are *New Jersey v. T.L.O.* (1985), *Bethel v. Fraser* (1986), *Vernonia v. Acton* (1995), and *Board of Education v. Earls* (2002). The decisions in these cases have given schools the power to curtail student speech, search students' belongings, and subject some groups of students to drug tests.

In *New Jersey v. T.L.O.*, the Court declared that the authority granted to school officials cannot be limited to their role as surrogate parents. In loco parentis confers only some, but not all, of the powers due to schools. Justice Byron White, the author of the decision, stated, "Today's public school officials do not merely exercise authority voluntarily conferred on them by individual parents; rather, they act in furtherance of publicly mandated educational and disciplinary policies." The Court concluded that although students have the right to bring personal property to school, their belongings (including the content of their lockers) can be searched if school officials have a reasonable motive, such as catching a student smoking.

The following year, in a decision penned by Chief Justice Warren Burger, the Court ruled that schools can suspend students who use lewd or suggestive speech. *Bethel v. Fraser* concerned a high school senior, Matthew Fraser, who gave a speech at a school assembly that contained numerous sexual innuendos and references, though none of the language was obscene. The Washington Supreme Court had ruled in favor of Fraser, but the U.S. Supreme Court overturned the lower court's decision and ruled on behalf of Bethel High School. Burger explained that "school authorities [can act] in loco parentis, to protect children—especially in a captive audience—from exposure to sexually explicit, indecent, or lewd speech."

The Supreme Court has ruled that schools have the right to protect students not only from indecency, but also from potentially unhealthy behavior. Specifically, they can conduct drug testing of students who participate in extracurricular activities. In *Vernonia School District v. Acton* (1995), the Court found that student athletes do not have the right to refuse to take a drug test and used the doctrine of in loco parentis to support its conclusion. Justice Antonin Scalia, who wrote the ruling, explained, "We have acknowledged that for many purposes 'school authorities ac[t] in loco parentis.' . . . Thus, while children assuredly do not 'shed their constitutional rights . . . at the schoolhouse gate,' . . . the nature of those rights is what is appropriate for children in school."

A subsequent decision, *Board of Education of Independent School District No. 92 v. Earls* (2002), expanded the *Vernonia* ruling; the Supreme Court declared that students participating in any extracurricular activity, athletic or otherwise, could be subject to random drug tests. Justice Clarence Thomas, the author of the opinion, also referred to in loco parentis in his argument:

> Today's public expects its schools not simply to teach the fundamentals, but 'to shoulder the burden of feeding students breakfast and lunch, offering before and after school child care services, and providing medical and psychological services,' all in a school environment that is safe and encourages learning. . . . The law itself recognizes these responsibilities with the phrase in loco parentis—a phrase . . . which reflects, not that a child or adolescent lacks an interest in privacy, but that a child's or adolescent's school-related privacy interest, when compared to the privacy interests of an adult, has different dimensions.

The Supreme Court's ruling in *Board of Education v. Earls* was criticized on both sides of the political spectrum. Conservative columnist Debra Saunders writes in a column for Townhall.com, "Before, parents were free to drug test their children, if they chose. Now the highest court in the land says that schools have a pre-eminent role in those personal decisions, and parents who want their kids to participate in important extra-curricular activities can't, well, just say no." Peter Cassidy, writing for the alternative media Web site Alternet, echoes Saunders's sentiments, writing, "Justice Thomas transformed the obligations of in loco parentis that are delegated to schools by parents into a discrete new authority all its own—one that supercedes fourth amendment considerations and the parents' sentiments as well." They and other commentators believe that the right of schools to make decisions in the place of parents does not mean that parental beliefs should be overruled.

Although not every court case regarding students' rights hinges on the in loco parentis doctrine, those three words have significantly shaped the legal position of American students. For nearly four decades the Supreme Court and lower courts have reevaluated the constitutional rights of students. In *Issues on Trial: Students' Rights,* justices and commentators debate the freedoms of students through the following cases: *New Jersey v. T.L.O., Hazelwood School District v. Kuhlmeier, Vernonia School District v. Acton,* and *Michael A. Newdow v. U.S. Congress et al.* The decisions in these cases show that whether they are at home or at school, American teenagers do not have the same rights as adults.

CHAPTER 1

The Right of Schools to Search Students

Case Overview

New Jersey v. T.L.O. (1985)

The Fourth Amendment to the Constitution declares in part that Americans are protected against "unreasonable searches and seizures." The Supreme Court has repeatedly considered how best to define "unreasonable," including in the 1985 case *New Jersey v. T.L.O.* The case had its origins in 1980, when a teacher at Piscataway High School in Middlesex County, New Jersey, found two girls smoking in a bathroom. The girls, including T.L.O. (a freshman whose identity has been protected), were taken to the principal's office, where the assistant vice principal, Theodore Choplick, demanded to see the contents of T.L.O.'s purse. In his search he found that the purse contained not only cigarettes, but also rolling papers, a small amount of marijuana, and a variety of materials that suggested T.L.O. was dealing marijuana to other students. T.L.O. confessed to the crime but later charged that the search of her purse violated her Fourth Amendment rights.

The Juvenile Court concluded that the search was not unconstitutional, a decision supported by the Appellate Division of the New Jersey Superior Court. However, the decision was appealed to the New Jersey Supreme Court, which found that the search was unreasonable and ordered that the evidence found in the purse be suppressed. The state of New Jersey then appealed the ruling to the U.S. Supreme Court. In its decision, issued on January 15, 1985, the Court reversed the New Jersey court's ruling. According to the Supreme Court, in a decision written by Byron White, while students do have legitimate rights to privacy and are entitled to bring personal effects to school, the assistant vice principal had a reasonable motive to search T.L.O.'s purse. The fact that she was smoking meant that it was likely she possessed cigarettes, and the further discovery of rolling papers made it plausible that she participated in drug-related activities and thus justified a more complete search of her purse.

The *T.L.O.* decision has led to increased searches of students and their possessions, including the contents of their lockers, on the grounds that such searches help protect students from drug use and school violence. Consequently, it is one of the more important decisions made by the Supreme Court on the issue of students' rights.

> *"The reasonableness standard should en-*
> *sure that the interests of students will be*
> *invaded no more than is necessary to*
> *achieve the legitimate end of preserving*
> *order in the schools."*

The Court's Decision: Allowing Reasonable Searches of Students' Property

Byron White

School officials have the right to search student property if they
believe it provides proof of a crime, Byron White declares in the
majority opinion for New Jersey v. T.L.O. *White argues that the*
assistant vice principal at a New Jersey high school had reason-
able cause to search the purse of T.L.O, a freshman, after a
teacher discovered her smoking in a girls' bathroom. He notes
that students do have a right to privacy but contends that the
discovery of cigarettes and rolling papers typically used with
marijuana justified a further search of T.L.O.'s possessions that
was not a violation of the student's Fourth Amendment protec-
tion against unreasonable searches. White was a Supreme Court
justice from 1962 until 1993.

To hold that the Fourth Amendment applies to searches conducted by school authorities is only to begin the inquiry into the standards governing such searches. Although the underlying command of the Fourth Amendment is always that searches and seizures be reasonable, what is reasonable depends on the context within which a search takes place. The determination of the standard of reasonableness governing any specific class of searches requires "balancing the need to

Byron White, majority opinion, *New Jersey v. T.L.O,* January 15, 1985.

search against the invasion which the search entails." *Camara v. Municipal Court.* On one side of the balance are arrayed the individual's legitimate expectations of privacy and personal security; on the other, the government's need for effective methods to deal with breaches of public order. . . .

Expectations of Privacy

Of course, the Fourth Amendment does not protect subjective expectations of privacy that are unreasonable or otherwise "illegitimate." See, e.g., *Hudson v. Palmer,* (1984); *Rawlings v. Kentucky,* (1980). To receive the protection of the Fourth Amendment, an expectation of privacy must be one that society is "prepared to recognize as legitimate." *Hudson v. Palmer.* The State of New Jersey has argued that because of the pervasive supervision to which children in the schools are necessarily subject, a child has virtually no legitimate expectation of privacy in articles of personal property "unnecessarily" carried into a school. This argument has two factual premises: (1) the fundamental incompatibility of expectations of privacy with the maintenance of a sound educational environment; and (2) the minimal interest of the child in bringing any items of personal property into the school. Both premises are severely flawed.

Although this Court may take notice of the difficulty of maintaining discipline in the public schools today, the situation is not so dire that students in the schools may claim no legitimate expectations of privacy. We have recently recognized that the need to maintain order in a prison is such that prisoners retain no legitimate expectations of privacy in their cells, but it goes almost without saying that "[t]he prisoner and the schoolchild stand in wholly different circumstances, separated by the harsh facts of criminal conviction and incarceration." *Ingraham v. Wright.* We are not yet ready to hold that the schools and the prisons need be equated for purposes of the Fourth Amendment.

Nor does the State's suggestion that children have no legitimate need to bring personal property into the schools seem well anchored in reality. Students at a minimum must bring to school not only the supplies needed for their studies, but also keys, money, and the necessaries of personal hygiene and grooming. In addition, students may carry on their persons or in purses or wallets such nondisruptive yet highly personal items as photographs, letters, and diaries. Finally, students may have perfectly legitimate reasons to carry with them articles of property needed in connection with extracurricular or recreational activities. In short, schoolchildren may find it necessary to carry with them a variety of legitimate, noncontraband items, and there is no reason to conclude that they have necessarily waived all rights to privacy in such items merely by bringing them onto school grounds.

Striking a Balance

Against the child's interest in privacy must be set the substantial interest of teachers and administrators in maintaining discipline in the classroom and on school grounds. Maintaining order in the classroom has never been easy, but in recent years, school disorder has often taken particularly ugly forms: drug use and violent crime in the schools have become major social problems. . . . Even in schools that have been spared the most severe disciplinary problems, the preservation of order and a proper educational environment requires close supervision of schoolchildren, as well as the enforcement of rules against conduct that would be perfectly permissible if undertaken by an adult.

How, then, should we strike the balance between the schoolchild's legitimate expectations of privacy and the school's equally legitimate need to maintain an environment in which learning can take place? It is evident that the school setting requires some easing of the restrictions to which searches by public authorities are ordinarily subject. The war-

A narcotics dog inspects student backpacks. In 1985 the Supreme Court ruled that school officials have the right to search students' property. AP/Wide World Photos

rant requirement, in particular, is unsuited to the school environment: requiring a teacher to obtain a warrant before searching a child suspected of an infraction of school rules (or of the criminal law) would unduly interfere with the maintenance of the swift and informal disciplinary procedures needed in the schools. Just as we have in other cases dispensed with the warrant requirement when "the burden of obtaining a warrant is likely to frustrate the governmental purpose behind the search," *Camara v. Municipal Court,* we hold today that school officials need not obtain a warrant before searching a student who is under their authority.

Probable Cause vs. Reasonableness

The school setting also requires some modification of the level of suspicion of illicit activity needed to justify a search. Ordinarily, a search—even one that may permissibly be carried out without a warrant—must be based upon "probable cause" to

25

believe that a violation of the law has occurred. However, "probable cause" is not an irreducible requirement of a valid search. The fundamental command of the Fourth Amendment is that searches and seizures be reasonable, and although "both the concept of probable cause and the requirement of a warrant bear on the reasonableness of a search, . . . in certain limited circumstances neither is required." *Almeida-Sanchez v. United States* (Lewis Powell, concurring). Thus, we have in a number of cases recognized the legality of searches and seizures based on suspicions that, although "reasonable," do not rise to the level of probable cause. . . . Where a careful balancing of governmental and private interests suggests that the public interest is best served by a Fourth Amendment standard of reasonableness that stops short of probable cause, we have not hesitated to adopt such a standard.

We join the majority of courts that have examined this issue in concluding that the accommodation of the privacy interests of schoolchildren with the substantial need of teachers and administrators for freedom to maintain order in the schools does not require strict adherence to the requirement that searches be based on probable cause to believe that the subject of the search has violated or is violating the law. Rather, the legality of a search of a student should depend simply on the reasonableness, under all the circumstances, of the search. Determining the reasonableness of any search involves a twofold inquiry: first, one must consider "whether the . . . action was justified at its inception," *Terry v. Ohio*; second, one must determine whether the search as actually conducted "was reasonably related in scope to the circumstances which justified the interference in the first place," [*Terry v. Ohio*]. Under ordinary circumstances, a search of a student by a teacher or other school official will be "justified at its inception" when there are reasonable grounds for suspecting that the search will turn up evidence that the student has violated or is violating either the law or the rules of the school. Such a search will be permissible in its scope when the measures adopted are reasonably related to the objectives of the search and not excessively intrusive in light of the age and sex of the student and the nature of the infraction.

This standard will, we trust, neither unduly burden the efforts of school authorities to maintain order in their schools nor authorize unrestrained intrusions upon the privacy of schoolchildren. By focusing attention on the question of reasonableness, the standard will spare teachers and school administrators the necessity of schooling themselves in the niceties of probable cause and permit them to regulate their conduct according to the dictates of reason and common sense. At the same time, the reasonableness standard should ensure that the interests of students will be invaded no more than is necessary to achieve the legitimate end of preserving order in the schools.

The Legality of the T.L.O. Search

There remains the question of the legality of the search in this case. We recognize that the "reasonable grounds" standard applied by the New Jersey Supreme Court in its consideration of this question is not substantially different from the standard that we have adopted today. Nonetheless, we believe that the New Jersey court's application of that standard to strike down the search of T.L.O.'s purse reflects a somewhat crabbed notion of reasonableness. Our review of the facts surrounding the search leads us to conclude that the search was in no sense unreasonable for Fourth Amendment purposes.

The incident that gave rise to this case actually involved two separate searches, with the first—the search for cigarettes—providing the suspicion that gave rise to the second— the search for marihuana. Although it is the fruits of the second search that are at issue here, the validity of the search for marihuana must depend on the reasonableness of the initial search for cigarettes, as there would have been no reason to suspect that T.L.O. possessed marihuana had the first search not taken place. Accordingly, it is to the search for cigarettes that we first turn our attention.

The New Jersey Supreme Court pointed to two grounds for its holding that the search for cigarettes was unreasonable. First, the court observed that possession of cigarettes was not in itself illegal or a violation of school rules. Because the contents of T.L.O.'s purse would therefore have "no direct bearing on the infraction" of which she was accused (smoking in a lavatory where smoking was prohibited), there was no reason to search her purse. Second, even assuming that a search of T.L.O.'s purse might under some circumstances be reasonable in light of the accusation made against T.L.O., the New Jersey court concluded that Mr. [Theodore] Choplick [the assistant vice principal] in this particular case had no reasonable grounds to suspect that T.L.O. had cigarettes in her purse. At best, according to the court Mr. Choplick had "a good hunch."

Implausible Conclusions

Both these conclusions are implausible. T.L.O. had been accused of smoking, and had denied the accusation in the strongest possible terms when she stated that she did not smoke at all. Surely it cannot be said that under these circumstances, T.L.O.'s possession of cigarettes would be irrelevant to the charges against her or to her response to those charges. T.L.O.'s possession of cigarettes, once it was discovered, would both corroborate the report that she had been smoking and undermine the credibility of her defense to the charge of smoking. To be sure, the discovery of the cigarettes would not prove that T.L.O. had been smoking in the lavatory; nor would it, strictly speaking, necessarily be inconsistent with her claim that she did not smoke at all. But it is universally recognized that evidence, to be relevant to an inquiry, need not conclusively prove the ultimate fact in issue, but only have "any tendency to make the existence of any fact that is of consequence to the determination of the action more probable or less probable than it would be without the evidence." . . .

Of course, the New Jersey Supreme Court also held that Mr. Choplick had no reasonable suspicion that the purse would contain cigarettes. This conclusion is puzzling. A teacher had reported that T.L.O. was smoking in the lavatory. Certainly this report gave Mr. Choplick reason to suspect that T.L.O. was carrying cigarettes with her; and if she did have cigarettes, her purse was the obvious place in which to find them. Mr. Choplick's suspicion that there were cigarettes in the purse was not an "inchoate and unparticularized suspicion or 'hunch,'" *Terry v. Ohio*; rather, it was the sort of "commonsense conclusio[n] about human behavior" upon which "practical people"—including government officials—are entitled to rely. *United States v. Cortez* (1981). Of course, even if the teacher's report were true, T.L.O. might not have had a pack of cigarettes with her; she might have borrowed a cigarette from someone else or have been sharing a cigarette with another student. But the requirement of reasonable suspicion is not a requirement of absolute certainty: "sufficient probability, not certainty, is the touchstone of reasonableness under the Fourth Amendment. . . ." *Hill v. California* (1971). Because the hypothesis that T.L.O. was carrying cigarettes in her purse was itself not unreasonable, it is irrelevant that other hypotheses were also consistent with the teacher's accusation. Accordingly, it cannot be said that Mr. Choplick acted unreasonably when he examined T.L.O.'s purse to see if it contained cigarettes.

Search for Marihuana Justified

Our conclusion that Mr. Choplick's decision to open T.L.O.'s purse was reasonable brings us to the question of the further search for marihuana once the pack of cigarettes was located. The suspicion upon which the search for marihuana was founded was provided when Mr. Choplick observed a package of rolling papers in the purse as he removed the pack of cigarettes. Although T.L.O. does not dispute the reasonableness of Mr. Choplick's belief that the rolling papers indicated the presence of marihuana, she does contend that the scope of the search Mr. Choplick conducted exceeded permissible bounds when he seized and read certain letters that implicated T.L.O. in drug dealing. This argument, too, is unpersuasive. The discovery of the rolling papers concededly gave rise to a reasonable suspicion that T.L.O. was carrying marihuana as well as cigarettes in her purse. This suspicion justified further exploration of T.L.O.'s purse, which turned up more evidence of drug-related activities: a pipe, a number of plastic bags of the type commonly used to store marihuana, a small quantity of marihuana, and a fairly substantial amount of money. Under these circumstances, it was not unreasonable to extend the search to a separate zippered compartment of the purse; and when a search of that compartment revealed an index card containing a list of "people who owe me money" as well as two letters, the inference that T.L.O. was involved in marihuana trafficking was substantial enough to justify Mr. Choplick in examining the letters to determine whether they contained any further evidence. In short, we cannot conclude that the search for marihuana was unreasonable in any respect.

Because the search resulting in the discovery of the evidence of marihuana dealing by T.L.O. was reasonable, the New Jersey Supreme Court's decision to exclude that evidence from T.L.O.'s juvenile delinquency proceedings on Fourth Amendment grounds was erroneous. Accordingly, the judgment of the Supreme Court of New Jersey is Reversed.

> "The rule the Court adopts today is so open-ended that it may make the Fourth Amendment virtually meaningless in the school context."

Dissenting Opinion: Student Searches Must Be Based on Probable Cause

John Paul Stevens

The assistant vice principal at a New Jersey high school violated the Fourth Amendment rights of the student known as T.L.O. when he searched her purse and found evidence that she was dealing marijuana, Justice John Paul Stevens maintains in his dissent in New Jersey v. T.L.O. *According to the justice, the search violated the student's right to privacy as well as her constitutional protection against "unreasonable searches and seizures," as stated in the Fourth Amendment. Stevens argues that the school official overreacted to a minor infraction of school rules (smoking in a bathroom) and did not have probable cause to search T.L.O.'s purse. Stevens has served on the Supreme Court since 1975.*

The question the Court decides today—whether [assistant vice principal] Mr. [Theodore] Choplick's search of T.L.O.'s purse violated the Fourth Amendment—was not raised by the State's petition for writ of certiorari. That petition only raised one question: "Whether the Fourth Amendment's exclusionary rule applies to searches made by public school officials and teachers in school." The State quite properly declined to submit the former question because "[it] did not wish to

John Paul Stevens, dissenting opinion, *New Jersey v. T.L.O.,* January 15, 1985.

present what might appear to be solely a factual dispute to this Court." Since this Court has twice had the threshold question argued, I believe that it should expressly consider the merits of the New Jersey Supreme Court's ruling that the exclusionary rule applies.

Applying the Exclusionary Rule

The New Jersey Supreme Court's holding on this question is plainly correct. As the state court noted, this case does not involve the use of evidence in a school disciplinary proceeding; the juvenile proceedings brought against T.L.O. involved a charge that would have been a criminal offense if committed by an adult. Accordingly, the exclusionary rule issue decided by that court and later presented to this Court concerned only the use in a criminal proceeding of evidence obtained in a search conducted by a public school administrator.

Having confined the issue to the law enforcement context, the New Jersey court then reasoned that this Court's cases have made it quite clear that the exclusionary rule is equally applicable "whether the public official who illegally obtained the evidence was a municipal inspector, *See v. Seattle* (1963); *Camara v. Municipal Court*, (1967); a firefighter, *Michigan v. Tyler* (1978); or a school administrator or law enforcement official." It correctly concluded "that if an official search violates constitutional rights, the evidence is not admissible in criminal proceedings." . . .

Schools are places where we inculcate the values essential to the meaningful exercise of rights and responsibilities by a self-governing citizenry. If the Nation's students can be convicted through the use of arbitrary methods destructive of personal liberty, they cannot help but feel that they have been dealt with unfairly. The application of the exclusionary rule in criminal proceedings arising from illegal school searches makes an important statement to young people that "our society attaches serious consequences to a violation of constitutional rights," [*Stone v. Powell*] and that this is a principle of "liberty and justice for all."

Thus, the simple and correct answer to the question presented by the State's petition for certiorari would have required affirmance of a state court's judgment suppressing evidence. That result would have been dramatically out of character for a Court that not only grants prosecutors relief from suppression orders with distressing regularity, but also is prone to rely on grounds not advanced by the parties in order to protect evidence from exclusion. In characteristic disregard of the doctrine of judicial restraint, the Court avoided that result in this case by ordering reargument and directing the parties to address a constitutional question that the parties, with good reason, had not asked the Court to decide. Because judicial activism undermines the Court's power to perform its central mission in a legitimate way, I dissented from the reargument order. I have not modified the views expressed in that dissent, but since the majority has brought the question before us, I shall explain why I believe the Court has misapplied the standard of reasonableness embodied in the Fourth Amendment.

Evaluating the Reasonableness of Searches

The search of a young woman's purse by a school administrator is a serious invasion of her legitimate expectations of privacy. A purse "is a common repository for one's personal effects and therefore is inevitably associated with the expectation of privacy." *Arkansas v. Sanders* (1979). Although such expectations must sometimes yield to the legitimate requirements of government, in assessing the constitutionality of a warrantless search, our decision must be guided by the language of the Fourth Amendment: "The right of the people to be secure in their persons, houses, papers and effects, against unreasonable searches and seizures, shall not be violated. . . ." In order to evaluate the reasonableness of such searches, "it is necessary 'first to focus upon the governmental interest which allegedly justifies official intrusion upon the constitutionally protected interests of the private citizen,' for there is 'no ready test for determining reasonableness other than by balancing the need to search [or seize] against the invasion which the search [or seizure] entails.'" *Terry v. Ohio* (1968) (quoting *Camara v. Municipal Court* (1967)).

The "limited search for weapons" in *Terry* was justified by the "immediate interest of the police officer in taking steps to assure himself that the person with whom he is dealing is not armed with a weapon that could unexpectedly and fatally be used against him." When viewed from the institutional perspective, "the substantial need of teachers and administrators for freedom to maintain order in the schools" (majority opinion) is no less acute. Violent, unlawful, or seriously disruptive conduct is fundamentally inconsistent with the principal function of teaching institutions which is to educate young people and prepare them for citizenship. When such conduct occurs amidst a sizable group of impressionable young people, it creates an explosive atmosphere that requires a prompt and effective response.

Setting Lower Standards

Thus, warrantless searches of students by school administrators are reasonable when undertaken for those purposes. But the majority's statement of the standard for evaluating the reasonableness of such searches is not suitably adapted to that end. The majority holds that "a search of a student by a teacher or other school official will be 'justified at its inception' when there are reasonable grounds for suspecting that the search will turn up evidence that the student has violated or is violating either the law or the rules of the school." This standard will permit teachers and school administrators to search students when they suspect that the search will reveal evidence of even the most trivial school regulation or precatory guideline for student behavior. The Court's standard for deciding whether a search is justified "at its inception" treats all violations of the rules of the school as though they were fungible. For the Court, a search for curlers and sunglasses in order to enforce the school dress code is apparently just as important as a search for evidence of heroin addiction or violent gang activity.

The majority, however, does not contend that school administrators have a compelling need to search students in order to achieve optimum enforcement of minor school regulations. To the contrary, when minor violations are involved, there is every indication that the informal school disciplinary process, with only minimum requirements of due process, can function effectively without the power to search for enough evidence to prove a criminal case. . . .

A Trivial Offense

The Court embraces the standard applied by the New Jersey Supreme Court as equivalent to its own, and then deprecates the state court's application of the standard as reflecting "a somewhat crabbed notion of reasonableness." There is no mystery, however, in the state court's finding that the search in this case was unconstitutional; the decision below was not based on a manipulation of reasonable suspicion, but on the trivial character of the activity that promoted the official search. . . .

In the view of the state court, there is a quite obvious and material difference between a search for evidence relating to violent or disruptive activity, and a search for evidence of a smoking rule violation. This distinction does not imply that a no-smoking rule is a matter of minor importance. Rather, like a rule that prohibits a student from being tardy, its occasional violation in a context that poses no threat of disrupting school order and discipline offers no reason to believe that an immediate search is necessary to avoid unlawful conduct, violence, or a serious impairment of the educational process.

A correct understanding of the New Jersey court's standard explains why that court concluded in T.L.O.'s case that "the assistant principal did not have reasonable grounds to believe that the student was concealing in her purse evidence of criminal activity or evidence of activity that would seriously interfere with school discipline or order." The importance of the nature of the rule infraction to the New Jersey Supreme Court's holding is evident from its brief explanation of the principal basis for its decision:

> A student has an expectation of privacy in the contents of her purse. Mere possession of cigarettes did not violate school rule or policy, since the school allowed smoking in designated areas. The contents of the handbag had no direct bearing on the infraction.

> The assistant principal's desire, legal in itself, to gather evidence to impeach the student's credibility at a hearing on the disciplinary infraction does not validate the search.

The T.L.O. Search Was an Overreaction

Like the New Jersey Supreme Court, I would view this case differently if the Assistant Vice Principal had reason to believe T.L.O.'s purse contained evidence of criminal activity, or of an activity that would seriously disrupt school discipline. There was, however, absolutely no basis for any such assumption—not even a "hunch."

In this case, Mr. Choplick overreacted to what appeared to be nothing more than a minor infraction—a rule prohibiting smoking in the bathroom of the freshmen's and sophomores' building. It is, of course, true that he actually found evidence of serious wrongdoing by T.L.O., but no one claims that the prior search may be justified by his unexpected discovery. As far as the smoking infraction is concerned, the search for cigarettes merely tended to corroborate a teacher's eyewitness account of T.L.O.'s violation of a minor regulation designed to channel student smoking behavior into designated locations. Because this conduct was neither unlawful nor significantly disruptive of school order or the educational process, the invasion of privacy associated with the forcible opening of T.L.O.'s purse was entirely unjustified at its inception.

A review of the sampling of school search cases relied on by the Court demonstrates how different this case is from those in which there was indeed a valid justification for intruding on a student's privacy. In most of them the student was suspected of a criminal violation; in the remainder either violence or substantial disruption of school order or the integrity of the academic process was at stake. Few involved matters as trivial as the no-smoking rule violated by T.L.O. The rule the Court adopts today is so open-ended that it may make the Fourth Amendment virtually meaningless in the school context. Although I agree that school administrators must have broad latitude to maintain order and discipline in our classrooms, that authority is not unlimited.

A Curious Moral

The schoolroom is the first opportunity most citizens have to experience the power of government. Through it passes every citizen and public official, from schoolteachers to policemen and prison guards. The values they learn there, they take with them in life. One of our most cherished ideals is the one contained in the Fourth Amendment: that the government may not intrude on the personal privacy of its citizens without a warrant or compelling circumstance. The Court's decision today is a curious moral for the Nation's youth. Although the search of T.L.O.'s purse does not trouble today's majority, I submit that we are not dealing with "matters relatively trivial to the welfare of the Nation. There are village tyrants as well as village Hampdens, but none who acts under color of law is beyond reach of the Constitution." *West Virginia State Board of Education v. Barnette* (1943).

*"With the ever increasing drug activity
and the carriage of weapons in today's
schools, expedient searches are necessary
to protect students and school employees."*

The Ruling in *New Jersey v. T.L.O.* Helps Protect Students

Camilia Anne Czubaj

*In the following viewpoint Camilia Anne Czubaj contends that
the Supreme Court's ruling in* New Jersey v. T.L.O., *which expanded the ability of school officials to search students, benefits
students and school employees by reducing the potential for drug
use and other illegal activity. She explains how students easily
participate in drug deals, even in classrooms, and thus drug use
on campus is a legitimate concern. Czubaj also argues that court
cases that have followed in the wake of* T.L.O. *further support
the claim made by the Supreme Court that school officials who
have a reasonable suspicion are justified in searching the belongings of students. Czubaj is an educator and a writer whose work
is used by American and international universities.*

A wadded-up looseleaf paper flew across the classroom. A
seemingly typical classroom disturbance; however, on in-
spection, the crumpled paper contained marijuana. A student
brushed up against another student en route to the pencil
sharpener. A drug deal was made. A textbook was passed to
another student; another drug deal. The teacher turned toward the chalkboard to write the lesson, a student jumped out
of his seat, and made a drop two rows to the right before the
teacher turned to readdress the class. A female student loaned

Camilia Anne Czubaj, "A Legal Analysis of School Searches," *Education,* vol. 115,
Summer 1995. Copyright © 1995 by *Education.* Reproduced by permission.

her make-up compact to a fellow classmate to primp. Beneath the make-up puff was the "hit." A student entered the classroom with a flannel shirt tied around his waist. One sleeve was full of snuff to be sold to classmates. During class changes eye contact is made to prospective buyers, hands pass behind the students or to oncoming students, making deals. Money is rolled widthwise, easily concealable in hands. A mere handshake can produce a drug deal, all under the supervision and eyesight of a teacher. In all the above actual scenarios, a warrant to search would not have been practical. Is it reasonable suspicion of an unlawful act to pass a textbook in class? Hardly so, yet drug deals are made in this manner during school hours. Most drug deals are not carried out in parking lots or school lavatories, but students make drug deals within the classroom. The teacher present. Some students attend school for the sole purpose of drug dealing where the potential customers are readily accessible and in abundance. School lavatories extrude smoke into hallways. Asthmatic students find it difficult to use the facilities. States are passing anti-smoking laws prohibiting smoking in and on all school premises. Metal detectors are being installed at school entrances in an attempt to curb the increasing weapon possession by students in schools. School searches produce evidence to the before mentioned illicit activities. Some school searches have been deemed unconstitutional by the court system. Many school searches have been upheld with the evidence obtained through school searches; the student being convicted of unlawful behavior.

Searches Under the Fourth Amendment

School searches fall under the jurisdiction of the Fourth Amendment to the United States Constitution.

> The right of the people to be secure in their persons, houses, papers, and effects against unreasonable searches and seizures, shall not be violated, and no Warrants shall issue, but upon probable cause, supported by Oath or affirmation, and

particularly describing the place to be searched and the persons or things to be seized.

The Fourth Amendment is used by courts to determine whether a school search was constitutional or unconstitutional. The U.S. Supreme Court case, *New Jersey vs. TLO*, tested the Fourth Amendment with a school search in 1984. *New Jersey vs. TLO* is the case subsequent school search cases use to uphold the legality of a school search.

The *TLO* Case

The U.S. Supreme Court case, *New Jersey vs. TLO*, was decided January 15, 1985. The case began in 1984 when a New Jersey high school educator discovered two female students smoking in the school lavatory, a violation of school policy. The student was taken to the assistant principal where the student denied the smoking charge. The assistant principal demanded to see the student's purse in which he found a package of cigarettes. Upon removal of the cigarettes, the principal found cigarette rolling papers and proceeded to search, discovering marijuana, a pipe, plastic bags, a large amount of money, a listing of students owing money, and two letters implicating the student in marijuana marketing. The state brought TLO to juvenile court. The court found the school official's search was reasonable and the Fourth Amendment did indeed pertain to school searches. The case went to the appellate division of the New Jersey Superior Court where the previous court's finding was upheld but supported the court's findings with other grounds than delinquency. The New Jersey Supreme Court found the search of the student's purse unreasonable and reversed the decision. The case then went to the U.S. Supreme Court.

The U.S. Supreme Court held the Fourth Amendment does apply to school searches. The rationale being school officials act as state agents enforcing state statutes as well as school policies. The second issue *New Jersey vs. TLO* dealt with was students' privacy. When students bring personal effects onto school grounds, students do have the right to privacy regarding their personal belongings. However, a "balance" between this privacy and the obligation of school officials to maintain an environment conducive to learning must be met. . . . An easing of the privacy restrictions while students are under school authority is warranted. Search warrants need not be obtained by school authorities prior to student searches. Also, school officials need not have probable cause in regards to law violations prior to student searches.

Determining Reasonableness

"Reasonableness" is the criteria for a student search. Reasonableness, as defined by the court, consists of two constructs: 1) justification at the inception of the search and 2) reasonable relatedness to the issue for which the search was implemented. A search by school officials is considered reasonable when suspicion will uncover evidence a student is/has violated the law or school policies. The court found such a search is permissible when related to the search objectives. The search should not be overly intrusive to the student's age and sex and the [nature] of the infraction. The third issue the U.S. Supreme Court addressed was the reasonableness of the search in *New Jersey vs. TLO* to the Fourth Amendment. The search of the student's purse was deemed reasonable due to the smoking violation in the school lavatory. After finding the cigarettes, the assistant principal then found cigarette rolling papers and continued his search disclosing the marijuana and other marijuana effects. The court found the assistant principal justified in his search of the student's purse. Justice [Byron] White presided over the case.

Courts must analyze each school search individually, examining the different circumstances related to the school searches and not apply *New Jersey vs. TLO* blatantly to every school search. In dealing with the Fourth Amendment, it must first be determined if a search did occur. If a search was not performed, the Fourth Amendment does not apply. A search is when a "government actor physically intruded into a constitutionally protected area," as defined in the *New York Law Review*. Justice (John Marshall) Harlan defined a search, pertaining to a search referred to by the Fourth Amendment, being composed of two constructs: a person must be expecting privacy in connection with the property that was physically intruded upon and society's schemata as to "reasonableness." There are two approaches to determination of reasonableness. The conventional approach to an unreasonable search rests without the issuance of a warrant deemed through probable cause. According to the *New York Law Review*, the Supreme Court, with few exceptions, generally adheres to the conventional interpretation to the Fourth Amendment in criminal cases. In the more contemporary interpretation of the Fourth Amendment, the warrant and the reasonableness are interpreted as two distinctive constructs. It is through the contemporary interpretation school administrations have been permitted to search students' belongings. The balancing test inferred by *New Jersey vs. TLO* elicits three possible court scenarios as a result of a school search: 1) a court may deem a warrant due to probable cause was necessary, 2) suspicion was justified without the requirement of a warrant, and 3) both the warrant and the probable cause are dispensed by the court.

Types of Searches

There are four types of school searches: 1) school and school grounds, 2) student vehicles on school premises, 3) out of school extra curricular activities, and 4) a student's vehicle located near to but off school property while the student is in school attendance or while a student is in transit to/from school. Greater privacy expectations are accorded the student as the student is removed from the structured school atmosphere. Warrants would be more applicable in the last three before mentioned types of school searches. Searches conducted in school and on school grounds include students, personal effects as well as school owned properties (lockers, desks, etc.), but does not include vehicular searches. It was felt reasonable to expect limited degrees of privacy in these types of searches due to the structured environment of the school setting and the proximity to vast numbers of fellow students. Several state cases concerning searches of lockers were upheld with *New Jersey vs. TLO*. School lockers and desks are not owned by the student, but merely loaned for storage purposes to students. Warrants to search school owned property by school officials is not deemed necessary. On campus vehicular searches have been tried using *New Jersey vs. TLO* without procurement of a warrant or probable cause. The *New York Law Review* chastised courts for not realizing the narrowness of *New Jersey vs. TLO*'s ruling as well as the courts neglecting to take into account the greater student expectation of privacy regarding their vehicles. It was stated, the school parking lot is not an environment conducive to learning as that of a classroom. Only one extra curricular search, thus far, has applied *New Jersey vs. TLO* in the justification of a hotel room search for alcoholic products. The initial search produced no alcohol, but a subsequent search of the adjacent hotel room produced beer and wine. School officials are deemed state agents during off-campus extra curriculum activities. Students in attendance at extra curriculum activities do not abandon the right to unreasonable searches: the students have a greater expectation to privacy. Expectation of privacy increases when the extra curriculum activity occurs after school hours. Probable cause should be the determining factor in extra curriculum searches. Searches concerning off-campus and non-school activity affiliation (vehicles parked near schools, transit to/from school, etc.) have thus far gone untested in the court system. It was felt both the issuance of a warrant and probable cause would govern such searches due to the student privacy expectations generated in such instances. Law enforcement officials can be notified to conduct such searches.

According to Professor Robert Berkley Harper, an important issue not argued in *New Jersey vs. TLO* was the element of suspicion in regards to the "unreasonableness" to school searches. Individual suspicion has been a prerequisite whereby adults have been stopped and frisked for weapons or tested for drug usage. Searches en masse by school officials have and continue to be conducted since individual suspicion has not been a component to school searches. Should individual suspicion be ruled an essential component to school searches in the future, emergency situations should permit school officials to waiver individual suspicion. A school search for a bomb, weapons, and/or drugs would necessitate the waiver.

Other School Search Cases

Many lower court cases have used *New Jersey vs. TLO* to uphold the constitutionality of school searches as well as validating the evidence obtained through the search as permissible evidence leading to the conviction of the offender. In *West Virginia State vs. Joseph T,* a student came to school smelling of alcohol at a fellow classmate's house prior to arriving to school. The vice principal ordered the fellow classmate's locker searched. Alcohol was not discovered, but in the student's coat pocket marijuana and drug paraphernalia were discovered. *New Jersey vs. TLO* was cited to uphold the legality of the search and illegal effects. A Californian student, Bobby B., was in the school lavatory where he was stopped by the school's dean and questioned. The combination of the student responding nervously and the dean's belief of campus drug use led the dean to ask Bobby B. to empty his pockets once they were in the privacy of the dean's office. Two marijuana cigarettes and cocaine (concealed in the wallet) were exposed.

New Jersey vs. TLO was cited again for both the legality of the search and the contraband. An informant told school officials [Christopher] Irby sold him marijuana in the case *Irby vs. State.* The school administrators searched Irby's belongings, finding marijuana in his coat lining. *Shamburg vs. State,* a student was suspected of being under the influence of alcohol (alcoholic aroma, slurred speech, glassy eyed, swaying). The school officials [searched the] student's vehicle and found cocaine in the student's ashtray. Both cases used *New Jersey vs. TLO* to win conviction of the students. Another case, *Burham vs. West,* allowed school officials to smell the fingers of a student in court. The court found the smelling of air space was within the legal rights of the administration. *West's Michigan Digest* lists two school search cases. The first case, *Cales vs. Howell Public Schools,* found the student's activity, ducking behind cars in the school parking lot during school hours, was not sufficient suspicion which led to the search that discovered drugs. The court ruled such activity would be more indicative of truancy or vehicular vandalism. A second case, *People vs. Ward,* upheld the student's search for drugs when the principal was informed by the counselor the student was seen selling pills on numerous occasions.

There must be reasonable grounds to conduct a school search with a legitimate goal as the end means. School officials no longer act as loco parentis, surrogate parents, but have been accorded the positions of state law enforcers. Many search cases do not go to court but are attempted to be resolved within the school settings, enrolling students into drug awareness programs. The cases concerning school searches that do go to court are upheld with the U.S. Supreme Court case *New Jersey vs. TLO.* With the ever increasing drug activity and the carriage of weapons in today's schools, expedient searches are necessary to protect students and school employees. Warrants and probable cause are not prerequisites to school searches when the safety for all concerned prevails.

*"Little if any Fourth Amendment protec-
tion now exists to shield students from
the raw exercise of police power in public
schools."*

Students Are Losing Their Fourth Amendment Rights

Randall R. Beger

The ruling made by the Supreme Court in its 1985 decision New
Jersey v. T.L.O. *has led to the gradual disappearance of students'
Fourth Amendment rights, Randall R. Beger charges in the following viewpoint. He maintains that the decision, which supported an assistant vice principal's search of a student's purse after she was caught smoking in a school bathroom, has led to a
rise in further invasive searches and surveillance. According to
Beger, although school violence has been exaggerated, students
continue to find themselves under the eye of police and security
guards, who repeatedly search students' lockers and personal
property. Such searches are unconstitutional, he argues, because
they are not based on probable cause or reasonable suspicion.
Beger is a professor at Harlaxton College, the British campus of
the University of Evansville.*

This article examines law enforcement expansion in schools
and the vanishing Fourth Amendment rights of public
school children. The climate of fear generated by recent school
shootings has spurred school administrators to increase security through physical means (locks, surveillance cameras, metal
detectors) and to hire more police and security guards. State
lawmakers have eagerly jumped on the school safety band-

Randall R. Beger, "Expansion of Police Power in Public Schools and the Vanishing
Rights of Students," *Social Justice,* Spring/Summer 2002. Copyright © 2002 by Crime
and Social Justice Associates. Reproduced by permission.

wagon by making it easier to punish school children as adults for a wide range of offenses that traditionally have been handled informally by teachers. Instead of safeguarding the rights of students against arbitrary police power, our nation's courts are granting police and school officials more authority to conduct searches of students. Tragically, little if any Fourth Amendment protection now exists to shield students from the raw exercise of police power in public schools.

A New Emphasis on Security

In response to the latest string of sensationalized school shootings, schools everywhere have made safety a top priority. A recent U.S. Department of Education survey of public schools found that 96% required guests to sign in before entering the school building, 80% had a closed campus policy that forbids students to leave campus for lunch, and 53% controlled access to their school buildings. A National School Board Association survey of over 700 school districts throughout the United States found that 39% of urban school districts use metal detectors, 75% use locker searches, and 65% use security personnel. Schools have introduced stricter dress codes, put up barbed-wire security fences, banned book bags and pagers, and have added "lock down drills" and "SWAT team" rehearsals to their safety programs. Officials in Dallas, Texas, unveiled a $41 million state-of-the-art "security conscious" school that has 37 surveillance cameras, six metal detectors, and a security command center for monitoring the building and grounds. At Tewksbury Memorial High School in Massachusetts, 20 video cameras bring the school into the local police department via remote access technology. According to one source [*Current Events*] "the video cameras record almost everything students say and do at school—eating in the cafeteria, cramming in the library, chatting in the halls." The new security culture in public schools has stirred debate over whether schools have turned into "learning prisons" [according to Gail R. Chaddock] where the students unwittingly become "guinea pigs" to test the latest security devices.

Since the mid-1990s, a growing number of schools have adopted zero tolerance policies under which students receive predetermined penalties for any offense, no matter how minor. Students have been expelled or suspended from school for sharing aspirin, Midol, and Certs tablets, and for bringing nail clippers and scissors to class. There is no credible evidence that zero tolerance measures improve classroom management or the behavior of students. Such measures are not only ineffectual, but also appear to have a negative impact on children of color. Research indicates that black children are more likely than are whites to be expelled or suspended from school under zero tolerance. Although most Americans believe that public schools are violent and dangerous places, numerous surveys on school safety contradict this notion. For example, according to U.S. Department of Education statistics, only 10% of public schools experienced one or more serious violent crimes during the 1996–1997 school year. Over the same period, almost half the nation's public schools (43%) reported no incidents of serious crime. Data from the Uniform Crime Reports show a decline of approximately 56% in juvenile homicide arrests between 1993 and 1998. In *Justice Blind? Ideals and Realities of American Criminal Justice,* Matthew Robinson explains why the conventional wisdom that schools are dangerous places is irrational: There are more than 51 million students and approximately 3 million teachers in American schools. In 1996, there were approximately 380,000 violent victimizations at school against these roughly 54 million people. This means the rate of violent victimization at U.S. schools is about 704 per 100,000 people. Stated differently, about 0.7% of people can expect to become victims of serious violent crimes at schools.

Police on Campus

The odds of a child being killed at school by gunfire during the 1998–1999 school year were about one in two million. Contrary to media hyperbole about violence in public schools, most school-related injuries are nonviolent in nature, and the majority of crimes that occur in schools are thefts.

Despite the relative rarity of school violence, officials everywhere are feeling pressure to improve the safety of students and staff. An increasingly popular "quick fix" strategy is to hire police and security guards. According to a U.S. Department of Education study, about 19% of public schools had the full-time presence of a police officer or other law enforcement representative during the 1996–1997 school year.

School police officers take many forms. Some are regular uniformed police officers working on a part-time basis for a school district. Others are hired and trained by school security departments. In New York City alone, some 3,200 uniformed school security officers work in the Division of School Safety of the City Board of Education, "a contingent larger than the Boston Police Department," [according to John Devine]. Many school districts use more than one form of police, such as campus police with support from local police or private security guards. . . .

Student Searches

Increasingly, the search efforts of police officials stationed in public schools mirror the actions of prison guards. For example, to create a drug-free environment, schools are allowing police officers to conduct random preemptive searches of students' lockers and personal property using specially trained sniff dogs. Over 1,000 schools in 14 states use drug-sniffing dogs supplied by a Texas company called Interquest Detection Canines. The profit motive is a powerful incentive to expand canine searches to schools that have no demonstrable drug problems. One school board has even formed a partnership with the U.S. Customs Department to send dogs into classrooms for drug-detection training exercises. In writing about canine searches in Boston public schools, journalist Marcia Vigue describes the following scene:

> Secrecy is the key. Students, teachers, and parents are not warned in advance; some student handbooks do not even explain that [searches] might occur from time to time.... During the searches the dogs respond to German commands like "sook"—which means search—by pushing their snouts against lockers and nudging their noses into bags and coats. Sometimes, after students have been told to leave, the dogs pass through classrooms and other rooms to sniff students' belongings.

The personal indignity of forcing students to submit to a suspicionless canine search is something no adult would tolerate.

Besides police controlled canine searches, schools are turning to sting operations in which undercover law enforcement officials pretend to be students to conduct actual criminal investigations of students suspected of using or dealing drugs in the school setting. In Los Angeles, for example, undercover officers made over 200 drug buys over a five-month period at local schools. Opponents of school-based sting operations say they not only create a climate of mistrust between students and police, but also put innocent students at risk of wrongful arrest due to faulty tips and overzealous police work.

When asked about his role in a recent undercover drug probe at a high school near Atlanta, a young-looking police officer who attended classes and went to parties with students replied: "I knew I had to fit in, make the kids trust me and then turn around and take them to jail" [according to Craig Schneider].

Police have adopted other aggressive search tactics on school campuses, such as herding students into hallways for unannounced weapons searches, known as "blitz operations." At Shawnee Heights and Seaman High School in Kansas City, signs warn students driving into school parking areas that they have just consented to searches of their vehicles "with or without cause" by school administrators or police officers. Scores of other schools across the country have adopted similar vehicle search policies. Groups of students have even been strip-searched by police officers to locate money missing from a classroom. There seems to be no end in sight to the aggressive search methods police are willing to use on students in the name of safety.

The Fourth Amendment and Schools

The Fourth Amendment of the United States Constitution provides the following:

> The right of the people to be secure in their persons, houses, papers, and effects against unreasonable searches and seizures, shall not be violated, and no Warrants shall issue, but upon probable cause, supported by Oath or affirmation, and particularly describing the place to be searched, and the persons or things to be seized.

In the past, courts held that school authorities acted in loco parentis when searching students and as such were not bound by Fourth Amendment restrictions that apply to state officials.

In the 1985 landmark case of *New Jersey v. T.L.O.*, the United States Supreme Court held that the Fourth Amendment did apply to searches conducted by public school officials. The Court specifically considered the search of a student's purse by an assistant vice-principal after a teacher had discovered the student, and her friend, smoking in the school washroom in violation of school policy. Upon searching T.L.O.'s purse, the assistant vice-principal discovered cigarettes and a package of cigarette rolling papers, which to him suggested involvement with marijuana. A more extensive search revealed a small amount of marijuana, a pipe, empty plastic bags, and letters implicating T.L.O. in selling drugs.

Thereafter, the police were notified and the state of New Jersey filed delinquency charges against T.L.O. for possession of marijuana with intent to sell. On appeal, the U.S. Supreme Court ruled that school children do not waive their Fourth Amendment rights by bringing purses, books, and items necessary for personal grooming and hygiene to school. However, a certain degree of "flexibility" in school searches was deemed necessary, which made the warrant and probable cause requirements "impractical."

Ultimately, the Court held that school officials need only have "reasonable suspicion" for student searches. Reasonable suspicion means that school officials "must have some [articulable] facts or knowledge that provide reasonable grounds" before conducting a search. Under *T.L.O.*, a search is reasonable if, first, the search decision is supported by reasonable suspicion and, second, the scope of the search is not "excessively intrusive" in light of the age and sex of the student and the nature of the infraction.

The *T.L.O.* decision avoided the issue of whether the probable cause or reasonable suspicion standard would apply to police searches in public schools. In the absence of a clear standard to guide police searches on school campuses, appellate courts have fashioned new criteria that give police officers the same search leeway as teachers. The case examined below, *People v. Dilworth,* is a good example.

The Kenneth Dilworth Case

Kenneth Dilworth, a 15-year-old high school student in Joliet, Illinois, was arrested for drug possession by a police detective assigned full-time to a high school for teenagers with behavioral disorders. Detective Francis Ruettiger served as liaison police officer on staff at the school, but was employed by the Joliet police department. Two teachers at the school asked Ruettiger to search a student, Deshawn Weeks, for drugs. The teachers informed Ruettiger that they had overheard Weeks telling other students he had sold some drugs and would bring more drugs with him to school the next day. The detective searched Weeks, but no drugs were found. Ruettiger then escorted the boy to his locker, where the youth and 15-year-old Kenneth Dilworth began talking and giggling. Ruettiger testified he felt "like [he] was being played for a fool." The officer noticed Dilworth had a flashlight and suspected it might contain contraband. He seized it, unscrewed the top, and found cocaine. After discovering cocaine, Ruettiger chased and captured Dilworth, handcuffed him, placed him in a police vehicle, and escorted him to the Joliet police station. Dilworth was subsequently tried and found guilty in adult court for unlawful possession of a controlled substance with intent to deliver on school property. He was sentenced to a four-year term of imprisonment. Dilworth's motion to reconsider the sentence was denied.

The appellate court reversed Dilworth's conviction on the grounds that his motion to suppress evidence discovered in his flashlight should have been granted. In the opinion of the appellate court, Ruettiger's seizure and search of the flashlight were based on only an unparticularized suspicion or "hunch" and did not comport with any standard of reasonableness for searches and seizures of students and their effects by state officials.

However, a divided Illinois Supreme Court in a four-to-three decision reversed the appellate court decision. Claiming that a flashlight in the context of an alternative school could reasonably be construed to be a weapon, the court affirmed Ruettiger's search as reasonable. The majority reasoned that lower expectations of privacy in the school setting, discussed in *T.L.O.*, supported a sharp departure from the probable cause standard for a school liaison officer. Even though detective Ruettiger was employed by the Joliet police department and performed duties at the school more in line with a regular law enforcement officer than a school official, the court maintained the search was proper.

The *Dilworth* decision stands in stark opposition to Fourth Amendment precedents that require the probable cause test to be met when evidence from a search by a law enforcement official forms the basis of a criminal prosecution. For example, in *A.J.M. v. State* (1993), the *T.L.O.* standard does not apply to a search by a sheriff's officer who was serving as a school resource officer and was asked to conduct a search by the school principal; in *F.P. v. State* (1988), the *T.L.O.* standard does not apply where a search is carried out at the behest of police.

Lowering the Standard for Searches

Justice Nickels, dissenting in *Dilworth*, severely criticized the majority for lowering the search standard for a school police officer when he stated:

> I cannot agree with the majority that a police officer whose self-stated primary duty is to investigate and prevent criminal activity may search a student on school grounds on a lesser Fourth Amendment standard than probable cause merely because the police officer is permanently assigned to the school and is listed in the student handbook as a member of the school staff. The majority's departure from a unanimous line of Federal and State decisions places form over substance and opens the door for widespread abuse and erosion of students' Fourth Amendment rights to be free from unreasonable searches and seizures by law enforcement officers.

The *Dilworth* decision is representative of a series of recent cases in which trial and appellate courts have lowered the bar for student searches by police officers. Instead of protecting schoolchildren from arbitrary police intrusion, courts have given law enforcement officials the widest latitude to search students. For example, state appellate courts have redefined police search conduct as "minor" or "incidental" to justify application of the reasonable suspicion standard (e.g., *K.K. v. State*, 1998). Appellate courts have also suggested that the lesser reasonable suspicion test should be applied when police search at the request of school officials or are present when school authorities engage in a search (e.g., *In re D.B.*, 1997). Courts have even upheld dragnet suspicionless searches of school lockers and police-directed canine searches of students' property with no warnings (e.g., *Commonwealth v. Cass*, 1998; *State v. Barrett*, 1996). Due to these decisions, public school children may now be searched on less than probable cause and prosecuted in adult court with the evidence from the search. . . .

Losing Constitutional Protections

Because the school setting demands "constant submission to authority" [as stated by Mai Linh Spencer] and is imposing harsher criminal penalties on students who misbehave, the legal rights of schoolchildren ought to be given the highest legal protection afforded by the nation's courts. Regrettably, the opposite is true. Bowing to public fears and legislative pressures, trial and appellate courts have reduced the Fourth Amendment rights of students to an abstraction. The nation's courts no longer seem interested in scrutinizing the specific facts surrounding the search of a student to determine if police had probable cause or even reasonable suspicion. Instead, courts search for a policy justification—e.g., minimizing disruptions to school order or protecting the safety of students and teachers—to uphold the search, even when police use evidence seized under lower and increasingly porous search standards to convict minors in adult criminal court. Given the current atmosphere of widespread fear and distress precipitated by the September 11 tragedy, there is little reason to expect courts will impose any restrictions on searches in schools.

Ironically, children are unsafe in public schools today not

because of exposure to drugs and violence, but because they have lost their constitutional protections under the Fourth Amendment.

> *"With respect to students' rights in school,
> the current juridical direction of Fourth
> Amendment law is of the most dubious
> legal, historical, and societal merit."*

Searching Students Is Not the Best Way to Reduce School Violence

Dorianne Beyer

In the following viewpoint Dorianne Beyer asserts that although some searches of students' personal property are justifiable under the Supreme Court's ruling in New Jersey v. T.L.O., *which declared that searching the purse of a student who was caught smoking did not violate her Fourth Amendment rights, such searches are not the best solution to school violence. According to Beyer, the rise in these searches is an indication that school authorities are increasingly unwilling to give students basic constitutional rights that most Americans consider inalienable. She maintains that there are better alternatives to reducing violence on campus, including law-related education, dress codes, and student courts. Beyer is the executive director of Defense for Children International–USA and a children's rights lawyer.*

The U.S. Supreme Court and state courts have very gingerly both bestowed and limited Fourth Amendment rights upon public school students in a series of cases over several decades. Recent cases may indicate that the delicate balance between student rights and school safety procedures is strongly tilting towards the rights of school authorities to proactively isolate and reduce perceived causes of school violence. Starting in 1968 and culminating in 1984, the law of the land concerning the status of students *vis-à-vis* school authorities shifted to a more constitutional basis. Prior to that time, student rights in school were defined by the common law doctrine of *in loco parentis,* which for centuries posited that school officials were given the right, duty, and responsibility to act in the place of a parent. Their right to act included the power to search students for illegal items, or for items merely considered to be contraband under state or local law or school district policies, without the warrant or probable cause prerequisites mandated for all other citizens under the Fourth Amendment. State laws, as upheld by their state courts, permitted such school action when, for example, student searches were deemed to be in the "best educational interests of all the students" (*New York Law,* 1978; *Illinois Revised Statutes,*1978). Any search based upon the much lower and non-constitutional standard of "reasonable suspicion" was found to be in accord with the doctrine of *in loco parentis;* it was accepted by the courts as necessary and reasonable in light of public necessity to maintain school discipline and order and the longstanding social concept of the parental powers of school authorities.

The doctrine of *in loco parentis* began crumbling in 1968, when *Tinker v. Des Moines Independent School District* (1969) found for the first time that constitutional rights—in this case, the First Amendment right to wear a black armband in school as symbolic speech in protest against the Vietnam War—were applicable to students. In landmark language that has been repeatedly cited, if not always upheld, the court said, "It can hardly be argued that either students or teachers shed their constitutional rights to freedom of speech or expression at the schoolhouse gate."

T.L.O. and Reasonable Suspicion

The question of whether Fourth Amendment protections

against unreasonable searches and seizures applied to students when searched by school authorities, and if so, with what restrictions, if any, was left unanswered by *Tinker*. It was not resolved until 1985, in *New Jersey v. T.L.O.* (1985). In that case, a teacher found a student (called T.L.O. in the case, to protect her youthful identity) smoking cigarettes in the high school bathroom, in violation of a school rule. When taken to the assistant vice principal's office, she denied the accusation and claimed she wasn't a smoker. When the assistant vice principal opened T.L.O.'s purse, he found not only a pack of cigarettes but also rolling papers associated with marijuana use. He then thoroughly searched her purse and found marijuana, a pipe, plastic bags, a large sum of money, a list of students who owed T.L.O. money, and two letters that involved her in dealing marijuana. When she was arrested on drug charges, she claimed that the evidence found in her purse should be suppressed as the fruits of an unreasonable search and seizure.

Since the Fourth Amendment only protects citizens against unreasonable searches and seizures by the government and its agents, there were two threshold questions to be answered. First, the issue of the application of the Fourth Amendment to students had to be resolved. It was decided that students subjected to school searches are, in fact, covered by the Fourth Amendment. For the first time, school officials were charged with acting in furtherance of publicly mandated educational and disciplinary policies that made them far more akin to government agents, the very subject of Fourth Amendment restrictions, than to parental surrogates under the doctrine of *in loco parentis* and free from constitutional restraints.

The next question to be considered was whether the search was reasonable, as guaranteed by the Fourth Amendment. As discussed, the Fourth Amendment requires a warrant and probable cause before a search is considered reasonable. However, there are several exceptions to the imposition of that formulaic and high standard. The *T.L.O.* court carved one such exception to the normal standard and found that the Fourth Amendment's requirement of reasonableness was met if school authorities acted without a warrant, but with

> reasonable grounds for suspecting that the search will turn up evidence that the student has violated or is violating either the law or the rules of the school. Such a search will be permissible in its scope when the measures adopted are reasonably related to the objectives of the search and are not excessively intrusive in light of the age and sex of the student and the nature of the infraction. (*New Jersey v. T.L.O.*, 1985).

In the *T.L.O.* case, all constitutional principles were found to be honored and the evidence of drug possession was admissible against the student.

Thus the "reasonable suspicion" standard was engraved in stone. It permitted school authorities to lawfully search students upon the passage of its two-prong test: the search must be reasonable in inception and reasonable in scope. . . .

Acceptable Searches

Some recent search cases in which the two-prong reasonableness test was successfully applied include:

- A school dance monitor, who, seeing that some students were inebriated, in contravention of school policy, took them to a private office and asked them to blow on her face (*Martinez v. School District No. 60, 1992*).

- Upon hearing an unusual thud when a student threw his bag onto a metal cabinet, a security guard rubbed his hand along the bag to feel for a gun (*Matter of Gregory, M., 1992/1993*).

- Upon a student's report to a guidance counselor that another student possessed an illicit drug, the administrator searched the latter student's book bag, because the administrator also had knowledge that the student had been previously disciplined for possession of a controlled substance (*State v. Moore,* 1992).

What cannot and will not be condoned by the courts are searches that are performed with malicious intent to deprive students of their rights, those where school officials know or should have known that their actions violated students' rights, those that are capricious or discriminatory, and those that do not closely follow school search policies. In *T.A.O'B. v. State* (1984), for example, a teacher who saw two students "exchange something" in an "off limits" area (although no sign or general student knowledge suggested the item was contraband), while one of them was holding an unlit cigarette (though no marijuana smoke or smell could be detected), claimed that he had fulfilled the "reasonable suspicion" test prior to performing a pat-down and wallet search of the student holding the cigarette, which did disclose the student's possession of marijuana. The court, however, found that the search was without reasonable suspicion, since the teacher could not articulate what school rule or law was being broken, nor could he point to any information that would lead a reasonable person to conclude that a search of the student's wallet would disclose marijuana. And, of course, no search is justified after the fact by any contraband it may reveal. An unconstitutional search leaves the school district open to civil damages for their violation of civil rights statutes, from which they are not immune. In addition, a school official who willfully violates a student's rights can be criminally prosecuted.

The case law on student search and seizure has yielded a few other useful factors to consider when conducting a search to ensure that it is reasonable at the inception and in scope. They include the student's age, history, and school record; the prevalence and seriousness of the suspected infraction or crime as a pervasive school problem; the exigency requiring the search without delay; the school official's prior experience with the student, and the evidentiary value and reliability of the information used to justify the search.

Various Types of Searches

The following sections outline the more common types of searches conducted in schools.

School Locker Searches. Most legal authorities state that the validity of locker searches is dependent on the students' reasonable expectations of privacy, which can be affected by school policies designating the lockers as student or school property, and student notification that the school will conduct periodic searches for contraband or will retain a master key to the locker for spot checks. The theory posits that unless school districts have written and distributed a locker policy to students, students may have a high expectation of privacy and school authorities may have to meet higher constitutional standards to conduct a locker search. The reality is that the courts have rarely found a school locker search they didn't like, as their application of *T.L.O.*'s "reasonable in light of all the circumstances" test has allowed state courts to override whatever expectation of privacy other citizens may have in similar circumstances. There is utter certainty that state law, school district regulations, or written school policies that require schools to maintain custodianship over lockers and to inform students of this policy in writing will override any student privacy concerns that could theoretically be asserted to disallow a search.

Vehicle Searches. Common sense might lead to the conclusion that the law of vehicle searches is quite different, since students' cars are certainly not school property under any theory. However, they still yield their secrets in the face of *T.L.O.*'s reasonableness test. In *State v. Slattery* (1990) for example, the court found it reasonable for an administrator, acting on a tip that a student was selling marijuana out of his car

in the school parking lot, to search the student's clothing. After a large amount of cash in small bills and pieces of paper
with a telephone pager number written on them were found,
school security guards were called in, who found nothing in
the student's locker. Next, the security officer searched the
student's car, and found a pager and a notebook containing
notations of names and dollar amounts. The security officer
then proceeded to open the car trunk and a locked briefcase
found inside it, discovering over 80 grams of marijuana. Although the student objected to the search of his car and locked
briefcase, the court found that the need to make the search
without delay, in addition to other factors, made it logical and
constitutional for the school to immediately search the car
and briefcase.

Similar to distributing a policy regarding school lockers, it
is helpful for school districts to establish student parking as a
privilege, not a right, and to require a pass or permit, which
clearly states the vehicle search policy or indicates student
consent to a vehicle search. A distillation of the case law and
commentaries results in the conclusion that vehicles parked
on school property can be searched if the searches are in compliance with the *T.L.O.* standards. However, for cars parked
elsewhere, law enforcement officers should be called in to perform the search.

Searches by Metal Detector Machines. A more common school
security procedure is the placement of metal detectors at the
school entrance or elsewhere on school grounds, in a general-
ized or mass "search" for weapons. It is exactly the non-
differentiation of an entry door or similarly placed metal detector search, as opposed to an individualized search, that
raises constitutional issues about compliance with the common sense definition of the required "reasonable suspicion."
In essence, can suspicions about a mass, undifferentiated group
ever be "reasonable"? Students do have reasonable expectations of privacy and, as they must bring many personal be-

longings to school every day—keys, money, and grooming aids, for example—it would be unreasonable for courts or legislatures to hold that students lose all expectations of privacy as to their property merely because they bring it into school. Thus far, however, at least three states (Tennessee, Louisiana, and Florida) have legislated permission for the use of random, nontargeted, mass metal detector use. Judicially, there have been only a handful of cases on this issue and none have been on the Federal level. They do, however, indicate a similar direction to permit non-individualized searches by metal detector. One theory holds that such a search is really an "administrative search," much like airport security metal detector use (*People v. Dukes*, 1992). Under the "administrative search" doctrine, such searches are reasonable as part of a regulatory, scheme in furtherance of an administrative purpose, rather than as part of a criminal investigation to secure evidence of crime. Other courts generally recognize a balancing test, weighing the privacy interests of the affected citizens against the government's need to conduct the suspicionless search and the extent of its intrusion. . . .

Alternative to Searches

With respect to students' rights in school, the current juridical direction of Fourth Amendment law is of the most dubious legal, historical, and societal merit. It highlights society's fears of and disrespect for children and the paucity of alternatives to police-type enforcement measures under consideration in the schools, and indicates that school authorities are no longer willing to grant students even a semblance of the civil rights and civil liberties the rest of the nation's citizens consider inalienable. The first line of defense of school administrators is to bring in more military measures, with car searches, metal detectors, urine analyses, and drug-sniffing dogs. The cases reported here, as well as many others not discussed, share a tenor of frustration and hysteria on the part of administrators to stop the violence and drugs, by any means necessary. What is also sensed in the many reported cases is that the only techniques tried were those of law enforcement.

There is, however, a wealth of information and experience about alternatives to police-type school violence prevention strategies. Law-related education (LRE) is a fresh approach to reducing the causes of school violence early and continually throughout a student's education. It is a generic, interdisciplinary direction to education combining particular kinds of content (related to rules, laws, and legal systems) with interactive instruction, adaptable to any grade level and intended to continue through all grade levels. The core of LRE is problem-solving, both as part of a group process and on an individual basis, since social conflict is at the core of both school violence and the legal issues that arise from it. Its aim is specifically to instill non-aggressive social problem-solving abilities, while also helping students become good citizens. Its method is to integrate into all curricula illustrations of common, student-relevant issues in the context of legal rights and responsibilities.

Law-related education is related to student conflict resolution and mediation training, including student courts. All of these initiatives provide early and constant education and experience, for grades K–12, in nonviolent means of violence prevention. Their programs and wide success have been well documented. Peer counseling has also proven effective in breaking the impasse between violent students and the school system. In a study of 600 Atlanta high school seniors and their parents by Emory University Medical School, 70 percent of the subjects said they would confide in a friend, more than three times the percentage who would confide in a parent, for example. Using trained students as helpers, friends, counselors, mediators, and educators to ease the school tensions and conflicts that result in violence is a more educational and effective first line of defense against school disruptions and crime than are police-type interventions.

The use of dress codes and uniforms to change a school's violent culture has dramatically reduced crime and violence in many school districts. Parental and other adult participation is also critical not only in contributing to and reinforcing school antiviolence programs, but also in aerating the school system and demonstrating that the entire community is involved in and cares about students education and progress. The list of alternatives to police-type interventions to combat school violence is, in fact, as extensive as society's creativity and commitment to empower rather than punish children.

Chapter 2

Limiting Students' Right to Free Expression

Case Overview

Hazelwood School District v. Kuhlmeier (1988)

The Supreme Court has repeatedly grappled with the issue of students' right to free speech since 1969, when it ruled in *Tinker v. Des Moines School District* that students have the right to express themselves as long as such speech does not substantially disrupt school activities. As Justice Abe Fortas famously declared in *Tinker's* majority opinion, "It can hardly be argued that either students or teachers shed their constitutional rights to freedom of speech or expression at the schoolhouse gate." However, nearly two decades later, the Supreme Court changed its view in its ruling on *Hazelwood School District v. Kuhlmeier.* The decision, penned by Justice Byron White in January 1988, asserted that school officials can censor school-sponsored newspapers without violating the students' First Amendment rights.

The *Hazelwood* case began in May 1983 at Hazelwood East High School in Hazelwood, Missouri. The school principal, Robert Eugene Reynolds, objected to two of the articles that were to appear in the next edition of the student newspaper, the *Spectrum.* One article concerned three pregnant students, while the other article described how divorce had affected Hazelwood students. Reynolds was concerned that the false names used in the pregnancy article would not adequately protect the students from identification; he also felt that the references to birth control and sexual activity were inappropriate reading material for the school's younger students. In addition he objected to comments one student made about her father in the divorce article, believing the parents should have been given the chance to respond to her remarks. After weighing his options and taking into consideration the fact that there was no time to change the articles before the paper was to be sent to the printer, Reynolds told the school's journalism teacher to remove the two pages that contained the stories.

Three members of the *Spectrum* staff brought a case to the U.S. District Court for the Eastern District of Missouri, arguing that their First Amendment rights had been violated. The court ruled that no such violation had occurred, stating that school officials can place limits on students' speech as long as their decision to do so has "a substantial and reasonable basis." The students then appealed to the Court of Appeals for the Eighth Circuit, which reversed the lower court's ruling on the basis that the *Spectrum* was a public forum that could not be censored.

That decision was appealed by the Hazelwood School District, Reynolds, journalism teacher Howard Emerson, and various school officials. In October 1987 the case was argued before the Supreme Court, which ruled to reverse the appellate ruling by a 5-3 vote. The majority opinion stated that educators do not violate the First Amendment when they control the content of school-sponsored student speech, provided such editing is done for legitimate reasons. According to the court, Reynolds's decision to cut the articles was reasonable and did not violate the First Amendment.

> *"Educators do not offend the First Amendment by exercising editorial control over the style and content of student speech in school-sponsored expressive activities."*

The Court's Decision: Censorship of School Newspapers Is Constitutional

Byron White

In the following excerpt from its decision in Hazelwood School District v. Kuhlmeier, *the Supreme Court rules that a school principal was justified when he ordered two pages of a student newspaper to be pulled because the pages contained objectionable stories on teenaged mothers and divorced families. Justice Byron White, who penned the majority opinion, asserts that the decision made by Robert Eugene Reynolds, the principal at Hazelwood East High School, did not violate the students' First Amendment rights because his editing had legitimate goals: to protect the privacy of the people described in the stories. White also maintains that the school newspaper, the* Spectrum, *cannot be considered a public forum and is thus not entitled to full First Amendment protection. White served as a Supreme Court justice from 1962 until 1993.*

Students in the public schools do not "shed their constitutional rights to freedom of speech or expression at the schoolhouse gate." *Tinker [v. Des Moines Independent Community School District* (1969)]. They cannot be punished merely for expressing their personal views on the school premises— whether "in the cafeteria, or on the playing field, or on the campus during the authorized hours"—unless school authori-

Byron White, majority opinion, *Hazelwood School District v. Kuhlmeier,* January 13, 1988.

Principal Robert Reynolds holds a copy of the school newspaper, Spectrum, *following the Supreme Court's ruling that gives school administrators wide authority to censor student publications.* © Bettmann/CORBIS

ties have reason to believe that such expression will "substantially interfere with—the work of the school or impinge upon the rights of other students."

We have nonetheless recognized that the First Amendment rights of students in the public schools "are not automatically coextensive with the rights of adults in other settings" [*Bethel School District No. 403 v. Fraser* (1986)] and must be "applied in light of the special characteristics of the school environment." *Tinker*; cf. *New Jersey v. T.L.O.* (1985). A school need not tolerate student speech that is inconsistent with its "basic educational mission" [*Fraser*] even though the government could not censor similar speech outside the school. Accordingly, we held in *Fraser* that a student could be disciplined for having delivered a speech that was "sexually explicit" but not legally obscene at an official school assembly, because the school was entitled to "disassociate itself" from the speech in a manner that would demonstrate to others that such vulgarity is "wholly inconsistent with the 'fundamental values' of public school education." We thus recognized that "[t]he determination of what manner of speech in the classroom or in school assembly is inappropriate properly rests with the school board" rather than with the federal courts. It is in this context that respondents' First Amendment claims must be considered.

Not a Public Forum

We deal first with the question whether [the school newspaper] *Spectrum* may appropriately be characterized as a forum for public expression. The public schools do not possess all of the attributes of streets, parks, and other traditional public forums that "time out of mind, have been used for purposes of assembly, communicating thoughts between citizens, and discussing public questions." *Hague v. CIO* (1939). Hence, school facilities may be deemed to be public forums only if school authorities have "by policy or by practice" opened those facilities "for indiscriminate use by the general public" [*Perry Education Assn. v. Perry Local Educators' Assn.* (1983)] or by some segment of the public, such as student organizations. If the facilities have instead been reserved for other intended purposes, "communicative or otherwise," then no public forum has been created, and school officials may impose reasonable restrictions on the speech of students, teachers, and other members of the school community. "The government does not create a public forum by inaction or by permitting limited discourse, but only by intentionally opening a nontraditional forum for public discourse." *Cornelius v. NAACP Legal Defense & Educational Fund, Inc.* (1985).

The policy of school officials toward *Spectrum* was reflected in Hazelwood School Board Policy 348.51 and the *Hazelwood East Curriculum Guide*. Board Policy 348.51 provided that "[s]chool sponsored publications are developed within the adopted curriculum and its educational implications in regular classroom activities." The *Hazelwood East Curriculum*

Guide described the Journalism II course as a "laboratory situation in which the students publish the school newspaper applying skills they have learned in Journalism I." The lessons that were to be learned from the Journalism II course, according to the *Curriculum Guide,* included development of journalistic skills under deadline pressure, "the legal, moral, and ethical restrictions imposed upon journalists within the school community," and "responsibility and acceptance of criticism for articles of opinion." Journalism II was taught by a faculty member during regular class hours. Students received grades and academic credit for their performance in the course.

Part of the Educational Curriculum

School officials did not deviate in practice from their policy that production of *Spectrum* was to be part of the educational curriculum and a "regular classroom activity." The District Court found that Robert Stergos, the journalism teacher during most of the 1982–1983 school year, "both had the authority to exercise and in fact exercised a great deal of control over *Spectrum.*" For example, Stergos selected the editors of the newspaper, scheduled publication dates, decided the number of pages for each issue, assigned story ideas to class members, advised students on the development of their stories, reviewed the use of quotations, edited stories, selected and edited the letters to the editor, and dealt with the printing company. Many of these decisions were made without consultation with the Journalism II students. The District Court thus found it "clear that Mr. Stergos was the final authority with respect to almost every aspect of the production and publication of *Spectrum* including its content." Moreover, after each *Spectrum* issue had been finally approved by Stergos or his successor, the issue still had to be reviewed by Principal [Robert Eugene] Reynolds prior to publication. Respondents' assertion that they had believed that they could publish "practically anything" in *Spectrum* was therefore dismissed by the District

Court as simply "not credible." These factual findings are amply supported by the record, and were not rejected as clearly erroneous by the Court of Appeals.

The evidence relied upon by the Court of Appeals in finding *Spectrum* to be a public forum is equivocal at best. For example, Board Policy 348.51, which stated in part that "[s]chool sponsored student publications will not restrict free expression or diverse viewpoints within the rules of responsible journalism," also stated that such publications were "developed within the adopted curriculum and its educational implications." One might reasonably infer from the full text of Policy 348.51 that school officials retained ultimate control over what constituted "responsible journalism" in a school-sponsored newspaper. Although the Statement of Policy published in the September 14, 1982, issue of *Spectrum* declared that "*Spectrum*, as a student-press publication, accepts all rights implied by the First Amendment," this statement, understood in the context of the paper's role in the school's curriculum, suggests at most that the administration will not interfere with the students' exercise of those First Amendment rights that attend the publication of a school-sponsored newspaper. It does not reflect an intent to expand those rights by converting a curricular newspaper into a public forum. Finally, that students were permitted to exercise some authority over the contents of *Spectrum* was fully consistent with the *Curriculum Guide* objective of teaching the Journalism II students "leadership responsibilities as issue and page editors." A decision to teach leadership skills in the context of a classroom activity hardly implies a decision to relinquish school control over that activity. In sum, the evidence relied upon by the Court of Appeals fails to demonstrate the "clear intent to create a public forum" [*Cornelius*] that existed in cases in which we found public forums to have been created....

The Right of Editorial Control

The question whether the First Amendment requires a school

to tolerate particular student speech—the question that we addressed in *Tinker* is different from the question whether the First Amendment requires a school affirmatively to promote particular student speech. The former question addresses educators' ability to silence a student's personal expression that happens to occur on the school premises. The latter question concerns educators' authority over school-sponsored publications, theatrical productions, and other expressive activities that students, parents, and members of the public might reasonably perceive to bear the imprimatur of the school. These activities may fairly be characterized as part of the school curriculum, whether or not they occur in a traditional classroom setting, so long as they are supervised by faculty members and designed to impart particular knowledge or skills to student participants and audiences.

Educators are entitled to exercise greater control over this second form of student expression to assure that participants learn whatever lessons the activity is designed to teach, that readers or listeners are not exposed to material that may be inappropriate for their level of maturity, and that the views of the individual speaker are not erroneously attributed to the school. Hence, a school may in its capacity as publisher of a school newspaper or producer of a school play "disassociate itself " [*Fraser*] not only from speech that would "substantially interfere with [its] work . . . or impinge upon the rights of other students" [*Tinker*], but also from speech that is, for example, ungrammatical, poorly written, inadequately researched, biased or prejudiced, vulgar or profane, or unsuitable for immature audiences. A school must be able to set high standards for the student speech that is disseminated under its auspices—standards that may be higher than those demanded by some newspaper publishers or theatrical producers in the "real" world—and may refuse to disseminate student speech that does not meet those standards. In addition, a school must be able to take into account the emotional maturity of the intended audience in determining whether to disseminate student speech on potentially sensitive topics, which might range from the existence of Santa Claus in an elementary school setting to the particulars of teenage sexual activity in a high school setting. A school must also retain the authority to refuse to sponsor student speech that might reasonably be perceived to advocate drug or alcohol use, irresponsible sex, or conduct otherwise inconsistent with "the shared values of a civilized social order" [*Fraser*], or to associate the school with any position other than neutrality on matters of political controversy. Otherwise, the schools would be unduly constrained from fulfilling their role as "a principal instrument in awakening the child to cultural values, in preparing him for later professional training, and in helping him to adjust normally to his environment." *Brown v. Board of Education* (1954).

Accordingly, we conclude that the standard articulated in *Tinker* for determining when a school may punish student expression need not also be the standard for determining when a school may refuse to lend its name and resources to the dissemination of student expression. Instead, educators do not offend the First Amendment by exercising editorial control over the style and content of student speech in school-sponsored expressive activities so long as their actions are reasonably related to legitimate pedagogical concerns.

This standard is consistent with our oft-expressed view that the education of the Nation's youth is primarily the responsibility of parents, teachers, and state and local school officials, and not of federal judges. . . . It is only when the decision to censor a school-sponsored publication, theatrical production, or other vehicle of student expression has no valid educational purpose that the First Amendment is "directly and sharply implicate[d]" [*Epperson v. Arkansas* (1968)] as to require judicial intervention to protect students' constitutional rights.

Reasonable Actions

We also conclude that Principal Reynolds acted reasonably in requiring the deletion from the May 13 issue of *Spectrum* of the pregnancy article, the divorce article, and the remaining articles that were to appear on the same pages of the newspaper.

The initial paragraph of the pregnancy article declared that "[a]ll names have been changed to keep the identity of these girls a secret." The principal concluded that the students' anonymity was not adequately protected, however, given the other identifying information in the article and the small number of pregnant students at the school. Indeed, a teacher at the school credibly testified that she could positively identify at least one of the girls and possibly all three. It is likely that many students at Hazelwood East would have been at least as successful in identifying the girls. Reynolds therefore could reasonably have feared that the article violated whatever pledge of anonymity had been given to the pregnant students. In addition, he could reasonably have been concerned that the article was not sufficiently sensitive to the privacy interests of the students' boyfriends and parents, who were discussed in the article but who were given no opportunity to consent to its publication or to offer a response. The article did not contain graphic accounts of sexual activity. The girls did comment in the article, however, concerning their sexual histories and their use or nonuse of birth control. It was not unreasonable for the principal to have concluded that such frank talk was inappropriate in a school-sponsored publication distributed to 14-year-old freshmen and presumably taken home to be read by students' even younger brothers and sisters.

The student who was quoted by name in the version of the divorce article seen by Principal Reynolds made comments sharply critical of her father. The principal could reasonably have concluded that an individual publicly identified as an inattentive parent—indeed, as one who chose "playing cards with the guys" over home and family—was entitled to an opportunity to defend himself as a matter of journalistic fairness. These concerns were shared by both of *Spectrum's* faculty advisers for the 1982–1983 school year, who testified that they would not have allowed the article to be printed without deletion of the student's name.

Principal Reynolds testified credibly at trial that, at the time that he reviewed the proofs of the May 13 issue during an extended telephone conversation with [newspaper adviser Howard] Emerson, he believed that there was no time to make any changes in the articles, and that the newspaper had to be printed immediately or not at all. It is true that Reynolds did not verify whether the necessary modifications could still have been made in the articles, and that Emerson did not volunteer the information that printing could be delayed until the changes were made. We nonetheless agree with the District Court that the decision to excise the two pages containing the problematic articles was reasonable given the particular circumstances of this case. These circumstances included the very recent replacement of Stergos by Emerson, who may not have been entirely familiar with *Spectrum* editorial and production procedures, and the pressure felt by Reynolds to make an immediate decision so that students would not be deprived of the newspaper altogether.

In sum, we cannot reject as unreasonable Principal Reynolds' conclusion that neither the pregnancy article nor the divorce article was suitable for publication in *Spectrum*. Reynolds could reasonably have concluded that the students who had written and edited these articles had not sufficiently mastered those portions of the Journalism II curriculum that pertained to the treatment of controversial issues and personal attacks, the need to protect the privacy of individuals whose most intimate concerns are to be revealed in the newspaper, and "the legal, moral, and ethical restrictions imposed upon journalists within [a] school community" that includes adolescent subjects and readers. Finally, we conclude that the principal's decision to delete two pages of *Spectrum*, rather than to delete only the offending articles or to require that they be modified, was reasonable under the circumstances as he understood them. Accordingly, no violation of First Amendment rights occurred.

The judgment of the Court of Appeals for the Eighth Circuit is therefore Reversed.

> "Official censorship of student speech on
> the ground that it addresses 'potentially
> sensitive topics' is . . . impermissible."

Dissenting Opinion: Schools Do Not Have the Right to Censor Student Publications

William Brennan

The following selection was excerpted from a dissenting opinion in Hazelwood School District v. Kuhlmeier *by Justice William Brennan who was joined by justices Thurgood Marshall and Harry Blackmun. Brennan contends that Hazelwood East High School's principal's decision to remove two articles from the school newspaper, the* Spectrum, *was censorship and violated the student reporters' First Amendment rights. According to Brennan, the Court's decision was not a legitimate abandonment of the precedent set in* Tinker v. Des Moines, *which gave students the right to express themselves as long as their speech was not disruptive. He explains that student speech cannot be censored simply because it deals with sensitive topics such as teenage sexual behavior. Brennan was an associate justice on the Supreme Court from 1956 until 1990.*

In my view the principal [at Hazelwood High] broke more than just a promise. He violated the First Amendment's prohibitions against censorship of any student expression that neither disrupts classwork nor invades the rights of others, and against any censorship that is not narrowly tailored to serve its purpose. . . .

William Brennan, dissenting opinion, *Hazelwood School District v. Kuhlmeier,* January 13, 1988.

Balancing Speech and Education

Free student expression undoubtedly sometimes interferes with the effectiveness of the school's pedagogical functions. Some brands of student expression do so by directly preventing the school from pursuing its pedagogical mission: The young polemic who stands on a soapbox during calculus class to deliver an eloquent political diatribe interferes with the legitimate teaching of calculus. And the student who delivers a lewd endorsement of a student-government candidate might so extremely distract an impressionable high school audience as to interfere with the orderly operation of the school. See *Bethel School Dist. No. 403 v. Fraser* (1986). Other student speech, however, frustrates the school's legitimate pedagogical purposes merely by expressing a message that conflicts with the school's, without directly interfering with the school's expression of its message: A student who responds to a political science teacher's question with the retort, "socialism is good," subverts the school's inculcation of the message that capitalism is better. Even the maverick who sits in class passively sporting a symbol of protest against a government policy, cf. *Tinker v. Des Moines Independent Community School Dist.* (1969), or the gossip who sits in the student commons swapping stories of sexual escapade could readily muddle a clear official message condoning the government policy or condemning teenage sex. Likewise, the student newspaper that, like *Spectrum,* conveys a moral position at odds with the school's official stance might subvert the administration's legitimate inculcation of its own perception of community values.

If mere incompatibility with the school's pedagogical message were a constitutionally sufficient justification for the suppression of student speech, school officials could censor each of the students or student organizations in the foregoing hypotheticals, converting our public schools into "enclaves of totalitarianism" [*Tinker*] that "strangle the free mind at its source," [as stated in] *West Virginia Board of Education v. Barnette.* The First Amendment permits no such blanket censorship authority. While the "constitutional rights of students in public school are not automatically coextensive with the rights of adults in other settings" [*Fraser*], students in the public schools do not "shed their constitutional rights to freedom of speech or expression at the schoolhouse gate" [*Tinker*]. Just as the public on the street corner must, in the interest of fostering "enlightened opinion" [*Cantwell v. Connecticut* (1940)], tolerate speech that "tempt[s] [the listener] to throw [the speaker] off the street," public educators must accommodate some student expression even if it offends them or offers views or values that contradict those the school wishes to inculcate.

In *Tinker,* this Court struck the balance. We held that official censorship of student expression—there the suspension of several students until they removed their armbands protesting the Vietnam War—is unconstitutional unless the speech "materially disrupts classwork or involves substantial disorder or invasion of the rights of others...." School officials may not suppress "silent, passive expression of opinion, unaccompanied by any disorder or disturbance on the part of" the speaker. The "mere desire to avoid the discomfort and unpleasantness that always accompany an unpopular viewpoint" or an unsavory subject does not justify official suppression of student speech in the high school....

Invalid Excuses

Even if we were writing on a clean slate, I would reject the Court's rationale for abandoning *Tinker* in this case. The Court offers no more than an obscure tangle of three excuses to afford educators "greater control" over school-sponsored speech than the *Tinker* test would permit: the public educator's prerogative to control curriculum; the pedagogical interest in shielding the high school audience from objectionable viewpoints and sensitive topics; and the school's need to dissociate itself from student expression. None of the excuses, once disentangled, supports the distinction that the Court draws. *Tinker* fully addresses the first concern; the second is illegitimate; and the third is readily achievable through less oppressive means. . . .

Official censorship designed to shield the audience or dissociate the sponsor from the expression [does not meet *Tinker's* standards]. Censorship so motivated might well serve . . . some other school purpose. But it in no way furthers the curricular purposes of a student newspaper, unless one believes that the purpose of the school newspaper is to teach students that the press ought never report bad news, express unpopular views, or print a thought that might upset its sponsors. Unsurprisingly, Hazelwood East claims no such pedagogical purpose. . . .

Educators Should Not Be Thought Police

The Court's second excuse for deviating from precedent is the school's interest in shielding an impressionable high school audience from material whose substance is "unsuitable for immature audiences." Specifically, the majority decrees that we must afford educators authority to shield high school students from exposure to "potentially sensitive topics" (like "the particulars of teenage sexual activity") or unacceptable social viewpoints (like the advocacy of "irresponsible se[x] or conduct otherwise inconsistent with 'the shared values of a civilized social order'") through school-sponsored student activities.

Tinker teaches us that the state educator's undeniable, and undeniably vital, mandate to inculcate moral and political values is not a general warrant to act as "thought police" stifling discussion of all but state-approved topics and advocacy of all but the official position. See also *Epperson v. Arkansas* (1968); *Meyer v. Nebraska* (1923). Otherwise educators could transform students into "closed-circuit recipients of only that which the State chooses to communicate" [*Tinker*] and cast a perverse and impermissible "pall of orthodoxy over the classroom," *Keyishian v. Board of Regents* (1967). . . .

The mere fact of school sponsorship does not, as the Court suggests, license such thought control in the high school, whether through school suppression of disfavored viewpoints or through official assessment of topic sensitivity. The former would constitute unabashed and unconstitutional viewpoint discrimination as well as an impermissible infringement of the students' "right to receive information and ideas" [*Board of Education v. Pico*]. Just as a school board may not purge its state-funded library of all books that "offen[d] [its] social, political and moral tastes" [*Board of Education v. Pico*], school officials may not, out of like motivation, discriminatorily excise objectionable ideas from a student publication. The State's prerogative to dissolve the student newspaper entirely (or to limit its subject matter) no more entitles it to dictate which viewpoints students may express on its pages, than the State's prerogative to close down the schoolhouse entitles it to prohibit the nondisruptive expression of antiwar sentiment within its gates.

A Vaporous Nonstandard

Official censorship of student speech on the ground that it addresses "potentially sensitive topics" is, for related reasons, equally impermissible. I would not begrudge an educator the authority to limit the substantive scope of a school-sponsored publication to a certain, objectively definable topic, such as literary criticism, school sports, or an overview of the school year. Unlike those determinate limitations, "potential topic sensitivity" is a vaporous nonstandard . . . that invites manipulation to achieve ends that cannot permissibly be achieved through blatant viewpoint discrimination and chills student speech to which school officials might not object. In part because of those dangers, this Court has consistently condemned any scheme allowing a state official boundless discretion in licensing speech from a particular forum. . . .

The case before us aptly illustrates how readily school officials (and courts) can camouflage viewpoint discrimination as the "mere" protection of students from sensitive topics. Among the grounds that the Court advances to uphold the principal's censorship of one of the articles was the potential sensitivity of "teenage sexual activity." Yet the District Court specifically found that the principal "did not, as a matter of principle, oppose discussion of said topic in *Spectrum*." That much is also clear from the same principal's approval of the "squeal law" article on the same page, dealing forthrightly with "teenage sexuality," "the use of contraceptives by teenagers," and "teenage pregnancy." If topic sensitivity were the true basis of the principal's decision, the two articles should have been equally objectionable. It is much more likely that the objectionable article was objectionable because of the viewpoint it expressed: It might have been read (as the majority apparently does) to advocate "irresponsible sex."

An Example of Brutal Censorship

The sole concomitant of school sponsorship that might conceivably justify the distinction that the Court draws between sponsored and nonsponsored student expression is risk "that the views of the individual speaker [might be] erroneously attributed, to the school." Of course, the risk of erroneous attribution inheres in any student expression, including "personal expression" that, like the armbands in *Tinker*, "happens to occur on the school premises." Nevertheless, the majority is certainly correct that indicia of school sponsorship increase the likelihood of such attribution, and that state educators may therefore have a legitimate interest in dissociating themselves from student speech.

But "[e]ven though the governmental purpose be legitimate and substantial, that purpose cannot be pursued by means that broadly stifle fundamental personal liberties when the end can be more narrowly achieved." *Keyishian v. Board of Regents* (quoting *Shelton v. Tucker* (1960)). Dissociative means short of censorship are available to the school. It could, for example, require the student activity to publish a disclaimer, such as the "Statement of Policy" that *Spectrum* published each school year announcing that "[a]ll . . . editorials appearing in this newspaper reflect the opinions of the *Spectrum* staff, which are not necessarily shared by the administrators or faculty of Hazelwood East," or it could simply issue its own response clarifying the official position on the matter and explaining why the student position is wrong. Yet, without so much as acknowledging the less oppressive alternatives, the Court approves of brutal censorship.

> *"The sad fact is that for many school offi-*
> *cials, their primary commitment is . . . to*
> *ensure that their school is portrayed in a*
> *positive light, no matter how unrealistic*
> *that portrayal may be."*

The *Hazelwood* Decision Has Lowered the Quality of Student Journalism

Mark Goodman

The decision made by the Supreme Court in Hazelwood School District v. Kuhlmeier, *upholding the right of a school principal to remove potentially problematic articles from the school newspaper, has led to increased censorship and harmed the quality of student journalism, Mark Goodman argues in the following article. He cites several examples of censorship of student newspapers throughout the United States, such as school administrators censoring an article about a teen parenting program. Goodman further argues that students who want to freely express themselves are turning to off-campus publications such as underground newspapers and online magazines. However, he notes, these publications often require financial resources not available to poorer students and are not supervised by experienced journalism advisers. Consequently, students are less able to learn about journalism skills and responsibilities. Goodman is the executive director of the Student Press Law Center, an organization that advocates for student free press rights.*

For most high school journalism teachers and publication advisers, teaching students to be responsible journalists

Mark Goodman, "Freedom of the Press Stops at the Schoolhouse Gate," *Nieman Reports,* Spring 2001, p. 47. Copyright © 2001 by Harvard University, Nieman Foundation. Reproduced by permission.

means instilling in them an unwavering commitment to the public's right to know the truth. In this time of moral ambiguity, that is a surprisingly easy sell to young people, who desperately want to believe their lives can make a difference. But teaching this lesson, which is at the very heart of the profession of journalism, has never been more difficult. The censorship faced by teen journalists and those who work with them today is constant and debilitating. The consequences, for the future of high school journalism and the entire profession, could be devastating.

Many who have not read a high-school newspaper in several decades may be surprised to learn how the medium has grown up. In 1969, the Supreme Court ruled that students had the right to wear black armbands to school to protest the Vietnam War. Students, the Court ruled, do not shed their First Amendment rights at the schoolhouse gate. As a result, public school officials were forced to recognize that some free press protections applied to the high-school media. By the early 1980's, courts across the country had ruled that unless public school officials could demonstrate some evidence that substantial disruption of school activities was imminent, they could not censor school-sponsored student publications simply because they were controversial or expressed unpopular views. As a result of these protections, the quality of high-school journalism soared as students began to discuss real issues such as teen pregnancy and school board policies instead of limiting their coverage to movie reviews and sports scores.

Censorship Emerges

In January 1988, the Supreme Court pulled the rug out from under the burgeoning success of the high-school press. In a case that arose from a school in suburban St. Louis, Missouri, the Court said that school officials had the authority to censor stories about teen pregnancy and divorce from a high school newspaper. In its ruling in *Hazelwood School District vs. Kuhl-*

meier, the Court said school official's have the authority to censor most avenues of school-sponsored student expression when they can show that their censorship is "reasonably related to legitimate pedagogical concerns." That phrase (Supreme Court legalese for having an educational excuse) dramatically lowered the First Amendment hurdle that lower courts had said school officials had to overcome before they could legally censor student media.

To no one's surprise, requests for legal assistance received by the Student Press Law Center (SPLC) in the years since the ruling have increased dramatically. In 1988, the SPLC received 548 calls for help from students and their advisers around the country. By 1999, that number had increased to more than 1,600.

The sad fact is that for many school officials, their primary commitment is not to teaching students the values of a democratic society or the principles of good journalism but to ensure that their school is portrayed in a positive light, no matter how unrealistic that portrayal may be. Censorship of the student media is one way they achieve that, as dozens of students and advisers tell the Student Press Law Center each month. Some recent examples:

- In Indiana, a principal censored a story that painstakingly described how freshman football players were threatened and beaten by upperclassmen as part of an annual hazing ritual. After the newspaper staff threatened to go to the local media, the principal allowed an edited version of the story to be published.

- In California, high school administrators censored a story about the growing popularity of "backyard wrestling," an organized effort by students to mimic television's professional wrestling matches, which sometimes results in physical injuries. Several months later, national newsmagazines were publishing stories about the phenomena.

- After a Florida student wrote a column criticizing the rap music industry for the role models it creates, her school principal prohibited her from writing any more articles for the newspaper because of her racial insensitivity despite the fact that she never mentioned race in her column.

- At a California high school, the principal censored a story about the school's teen parenting program because it would send the wrong message to the community. A neighboring high-school newspaper agreed to publish the censored story.

- After a Washington state student newspaper published a commentary criticizing the food in the school cafeteria, the principal prohibited the publication of anything "that is critical or might be perceived as critical" of any school staff member or program.

New Challenges

Students are not the only ones who are confronting this censorship. Increasingly school officials are threatening media advisers who refuse to censor their students as the administration demands. Thus advisers dedicated to strong and independent journalism may well find themselves confronted with the choice of protecting their students or saving their job. It's no surprise that the turnover rate among publication advisers is alarmingly high. Those who stay to fight for their students are true heroes.

Perhaps one of the biggest challenges to face the student media in recent years has revolved around changing technology. Teen reporters and editors, like their professional counterparts, have found the Internet an invaluable tool in researching stories and contacting resources. But the growing prevalence of filters on school computers has significantly limited its usefulness. Students and advisers report being blocked from sites dealing with topics like breast cancer and Bosnian war crimes because the school's imprecise filtering software excluded them. After one publication staff found that its school's filters blocked access to the Student Press Law Center's Web site, they persuaded school officials to provide them an unfiltered computer in their newsroom. Most students are not so lucky.

Moving into online publishing has also caused conflicts. Even schools that have allowed student editors to make their own content decisions for the print version of a student newspaper have censored an online edition or prohibited the publication from creating one altogether. The potential audience available on the World Wide Web makes some school administrators even more concerned about stories that could tarnish the school's image. Facing all of these threats and constraints, journalism educators are left to ask themselves whether we are really preparing students for their role as citizen defenders of press freedom. Or is the constant barrage of censorship teaching young people that there is nothing wrong with allowing government officials to dictate what is and is not news and that free expression is to be tolerated only as long as those in authority agree with it?

Alternative Forms of Expression

Despite increasing efforts to silence the student press, many students and teachers make their best effort to fight back. Many go public with their censorship battles, contacting the local media, in order to force school officials to publicly defend their efforts to silence student expression. Some students turn to their own independent means of publishing, through "underground" newspapers produced on a home computer and duplicated at the local copy shop or through an independent Web site. The courts have made it clear that school officials' ability to censor student publications distributed on school grounds that are not school sponsored is much more limited. And for publications created and distributed outside of school (independent Web sites, for example), school officials' ability to punish or censor student expression is virtually nonexistent. Parents, not schools, have the right to oversee student expression when it occurs outside the boundaries of the school day.

These off campus forms of expression are an important alternative for censored student journalists. But when press freedom is available only to those students who have the financial means to support it, the voices of poorer rural and urban students are lost. And the benefits of a trained faculty adviser who can teach journalistic skills, ethics and responsibility are missed when students are forced to turn away from school-sponsored media. Youth pages of community newspapers or citywide teen publications supervised by professional editors are a great training ground. But they can seldom reach the same number of students that would be involved in school-sponsored publications at each school.

Although the Supreme Court appears to have forsaken high school journalists, some legal protection against censorship remains. The most surprising response to the *Hazelwood* decision and the censorship it has inspired has been the effort to enact state laws giving students free press protections. The Supreme Court's ruling only dictated the limits of First Amendment protections; it left open the possibility that states could create their own laws or regulations that provide student journalists with greater rights than this high court recognized under the federal Constitution. A total of 29 state legislatures have debated such laws, and six now have them on the books. California, Massachusetts, Iowa, Kansas, Colorado and Arkansas have returned high-school journalism to the place it was before 1988, saying students will be allowed to express themselves freely in school unless school officials can demonstrate their expression is libelous, obscene or will create a substantial disruption of school activities.

Student Journalists Deserve More Support

One of the most frustrating aspects of this ongoing battle for many students and teachers has been how little support they sometimes receive from the local "professional" media. Most community newspapers and television stations have no idea if the high-school media in their community are being censored simply because they have never asked the students who produce them or advisers who work with them.

A high-school teacher's job was threatened several years ago because of a controversial feature published in the student yearbook on which she was adviser. "Why are they [the local media] so anxious to see us fail, highlighting what they perceive are our students' mistakes and never willing to defend our right to be less than perfect?" she asked. "Would they really like to be held to the same standard?"

She expressed a sentiment that discussions with student editors and advisers around the country suggest is sharply increasing. A growing number believe that the commercial media is only interested in the First Amendment and press freedom when its rights are being threatened and have little concern about those same rights as they apply to others, especially young people. After 15 years at the Student Press Law Center, I know that perception is not an accurate reflection of the attitudes of thousands of working reporters and editors at large and small news organizations throughout the nation. But I also know that most of these students will not make journalism their profession and thus will never set foot in a professional newsroom. Their attitudes about and the importance we place on press freedom will be fundamentally shaped by experiences that end the day they graduate from high school.

If we care about the future of journalism, we have to show student journalists that we care about them, too. Professionals who fail to defend student press freedom will have only themselves to blame when young journalists they hire are one day as indifferent to the First Amendment as many working journalists are now to the problems confronted by the high-school press.

School Newspapers Are Not Equal to the Real-World Press

Kevin W. Saunders

The Supreme Court was correct to rule in Hazelwood School
District v. Kuhlmeier *that school officials have the right to remove potentially offensive articles from student newspapers,
Kevin W. Saunders declares in the following viewpoint. According to Saunders, high school journalism is not entitled to the
same First Amendment protections as professional media because
high school students are merely journalists in training. Furthermore, he contends that high school newspapers do not play the
same role as those written by adults and should also be expected
to meet higher ethical standards than their more mature counterparts. Saunders is a professor of law at Michigan State University.*

There are two principles [guiding students' rights to free
speech]. The first is the recognition of the role of the
schools in educating the nation's youth and inculcating cultural values. That interest allows the schools to teach values
and to limit certain speech for two reasons. The first reason is
the disruptive effect the speech may cause, understood more
expansively than *Tinker*[1] might be read to include. The second

1. In *Tinker v. Des Moines Independent Community School District* (1969), a case that involved three students getting suspended from school for wearing armbands as a protest
against the Vietnam War, the Supreme Court ruled that censorship of students is permissible only if the school can show that the speech would be disruptive or infringe on
the rights of other students.

is the development of practices that society may consider positive in the adult world but cannot be regulated there due to concerns over abuse. The interests are, however, limited by a need for political neutrality in the schools, so that the majority does not use schools to limit dissenting views in the next generation on issues of controversy in the political community. . . .

High School Is a Training Ground

The other basis under which school authorities may limit student speech is explained by the "spring training" metaphor provided by John Garvey. As Garvey says, "[c]hildren are not full-fledged First Amendment actors. . . . Freedom of speech for children is instrumentally important, not intrinsically so—it is a right we protect in order to help kids become real First Amendment players." The fact that the real season has not yet begun for children allows differing treatment of their speech rights. Nonetheless, the government must exercise some restraint and recognize free speech rights that contribute to the child's development. Garvey, in an earlier article, offered several considerations in this regard. He discounts readings of *Tinker* that would give children free speech rights equal to those of adults, more limited only by the particular demands of nondisruption of the educational endeavor. Instead, he concludes that "the child's claim to recognition of such a right is valid only insofar as free speech is instrumental in the growth of his ability to participate in self-government." He also recognizes an interest in the search for knowledge and truth, but it is characterized as a training interest; that is, there may be no immediate good, but children's debates on adult issues train them for their future active role in the political community. The most significant restraint Garvey would place on the schools is that they not be allowed to subvert their own mission of teaching children to pursue knowledge.

Betsy Levin makes a somewhat similar point regarding the training interest in arguing that schools should be subject to First Amendment restraints. She recognizes the role of the schools in inculcating values but would give greater recognition to the expression rights of students. Otherwise, she says, "students will not come to an understanding of the value of a democratic, participatory society, but instead will become a passive alienated citizenry that believes government is arbitrary." Certainly, if the schools are too restrictive, this is a danger. While that justifies the imposition of some First Amendment restraints, it does not mean that they need have the same strength as in the adult world. While students must come to value democracy and participation, the extent of democracy and the nature of participation may differ in the two communities.

School Politics as Spring Training

Fraser[2] can certainly be seen as a spring training case. Student government elections are not the politics of the real season. They are the politics of the grapefruit league. It is not that they are not real but that they do not count in the world of real politics. The importance of elections for student leadership positions is not found in the issues of prom themes and the like that student government addresses. The importance is in the lessons provided in electoral politics. Student government leaders earn an item on their resumés that colleges, law schools and political organizations find valuable, but the value is not found in the fact that the prom was very popular and ran firmly in the black. Student government leaders do not rescue social security or reform health care. The value of the

2. In the case considered by the Supreme Court in *Bethel School District No. 403 v. Fraser* (1986), a student was suspended after using lewd language while nominating a fellow student for student government office during a school assembly. The Court ruled that the school made the appropriate decision, as it has the right to prohibit the use of vulgar language.

resumé item is the experience in getting elected, conducting meetings and working with others. It isthe exercise, rather than any result obtained after election, that is important. For student leaders, school politics is springtraining for later electoral campaigns or community leadership. For those not inclined toward leadership, school politics is still spring training for their role as voters in choosing leaders.

Since school politics is spring training, the rules may be different. They can be aimed at teaching lessons rather than solely at protecting the real political process. The government cannot insist on decorum in real-world politics; that would raise the specter of government suppression of positions with which it disagrees by finding the speech advocating the position uncivil. Schools should not face the same restrictions. The school may insist that candidates not campaign on the basis of how much homework should be assigned or the provision of free ice cream in the cafeteria. The school should be allowed to insist on campaigns addressing issues that student government is allowed to affect. Similarly, while the government cannot insist that real political campaigns restrict themselves to serious commentary on the issues and not use sensational speech, schools should be allowed more latitude. Spring training rules should allow the school to insist that nomination speeches present reasons why the candidate deserves support that are related to leadership qualities, rather than that the candidate is "firm in his shirt" and "firm in his pants."

School Is Not the Real World

Hazelwood can also be seen as a spring training case. The students in the Journalism II class were clearly in training, and school papers are to the outside world media what school politics are to real-world elections. Again, the major result of school newspaper work is a resumé item relevant to colleges and work on college newspapers as a step to professional journalism. Society cannot control the real-world press because of the danger of suppression of dissent. Indeed, society cannot even insist on evenhandedness in newspaper coverage. Nonetheless, fairness and balance are ideals to which the press should aspire and to which the culture, without official sanction, should hold the media. The same can be said of other issues in journalistic ethics, such as protecting the privacy of individuals when not central to an issue of true public concern. Concerns over protecting the role of the real-world press do not necessarily translate to high school newspapers. They do not serve the same essential role in preventing governmental abuse. They are training grounds for journalists and just as school elections can be idealized versions of real elections, school newspapers can be held to ethical standards one can only hope the real-world press will meet.

"Censorship of student expression, mainly in the form of publications, has only increased since Hazelwood."

Student Newspaper Censorship Has Been a Problem Before and After *Hazelwood*

Jeremy Leaming

In the following viewpoint Jeremy Leaming contends that censorship of school newspapers was a problem even before the Supreme Court's ruling in Hazelwood School District v. Kuhlmeier. *It has simply become easier for school officials to suppress students' right to free expression since the 1988 decision. However, Leaming adds, California and several other states have countered the effects of Hazelwood by passing laws that give student journalists greater protection against censorship—legislation that more states should support. Leaming is a contributor to* Freedom Forum Online.

It has been a decade since the Supreme Court significantly changed the practices of high school newspapers in this country by granting public school administrators greater authority to determine what kinds of student speech should be afforded a school audience. Prior to the 1988 Supreme Court decision [*Hazelwood v. Kuhlmeier*], however, public school students regularly faced school-sponsored censorship of their ideas. Indeed, censorship of student voices during the sixties and seventies rose to such a level that in 1974 a Commission

Jeremy Leaming, "Analysis of *Hazelwood*'s Impact on the Student Press," www.freedomforum.org, January 13, 1998. Copyright © 1998 by The Freedom Forum. Reproduced by permission.

of Inquiry into High School Journalism was created by the Robert F. Kennedy Memorial to determine whether First Amendment rights of public school students were properly protected. The commission's twenty-two members examined— through public hearings, consultations, surveys, content analysis and research—high school journalism. The commission undertook the study with the belief and "knowledge that high schools represent a significant contribution as well as an unfulfilled potential in America life."

The principles that led to the commission's formation and gave direction to its study centered on an appreciation for and an understanding of the First Amendment. Members of the commission knew that students' appreciation for the First Amendment would continue to suffer in an atmosphere where teachers would hail the values of the First Amendment and in the same instance suppress speech.

After studying several aspects of high school journalism, especially the impact of censorship, the commission issued a report in 1974, concluding among other things that "any censorship of journalism is a dangerous thing."

Censorship Before *Hazelwood*

An examination of the brief summary of the specific commission findings on high school censorship provides a good overview of the state of high school journalism before the *Hazelwood* decision. According to the commission's report:

1. Censorship and the systematic lack of freedom to engage in open, responsible journalism characterize high school journalism. Unconstitutional restraints are so deeply embedded in high school journalism so as to overshadow its achievements.

2. Censorship of journalism is a matter of policy, stated or implied, in all areas of the country, although in isolated schools students enjoy a relatively free press.

3. Censorship persists even where litigation or administrative action has destroyed the legal foundation of censorship.

4. Repressive policies are used against school-oriented media published off campus as well as within school.

5. Policies of censorship apply regardless of whether the material is substantive or controversial.

6. Even advisers or journalism teachers who in private favor a free student press often succumb to bureaucratic and community pressures to censor school newspapers.

7. Censorship generally is accepted by students, teachers, and administrators as a routine part of the school process.

8. Self-censorship, the result of years of unconstitutional administrative and faculty censorship, has created passivity among students and made then cynical about the guarantees of a free press under the First Amendment.

9. Fear of reprisals and unpleasantness, as well as the lack of a tradition of an independent high school press, remain the basic forces behind self-censorship.

10. Censorship is the fundamental cause of triviality, innocuousness, and uniformity that characterize the high school press.

11. Where a free, vigorous student press does exist there is a healthy ferment of ideas and opinions, with no indication of disruption or negative side effects on the educational experience of the school.

12. The professional news media does not take seriously the First Amendment problems of high school journalists and does little to help protect the press rights of students.

An Unclear Effect

The findings represented a substantial indictment against the state of high school journalism in America. The members of the commission hoped that their report would foster stronger support for high school students' First Amendment rights. It appears, however, that because of *Hazelwood*, the commission's goals remain unrealized.

Whether the Supreme Court's *Hazelwood* decision has actually spurred more instances of censorship is difficult if not impossible to document. Mary Arnold, a University of Iowa journalism professor and the executive secretary for the Iowa High School Press Association, notes censorship is nothing new to public education. "There really is no way to document whether censorship has in fact increased since the Supreme Court's *Hazelwood* decision," Arnold said. "In fact, many scholars try to start with such a premise but their outcomes ultimately prove disappointing, because really censorship has always been there." Mike Heaston, a lawyer for the Student Press Law Center, the only national legal assistance agency devoted to protecting and educating the student press, agrees with Arnold's assessment that it is hard to document the amount of censorship taking place on high school campuses. Nonetheless, Heaston said the number of calls the Center receives from students seeking help against threats of censorship has increased every year since 1988. In the year the Supreme Court handed down *Hazelwood*, the Student Press Law Center received a little over a hundred requests for legal assistance from high school journalists. By 1996, the SPLC reported a record number of requests by high school journalists for legal assistance. According to the SPLC, most of the students (37%) who called the Center sought help against threats of censorship.

The Supreme Court's decision, however, did significantly lower the First Amendment hurdle that school officials were once forced to clear before legally stifling student speech. For years prior to *Hazelwood*, public school officials had to prove a substantial disruption of school activities was imminent before they could legally muzzle student speech. In the wake of *Hazelwood*, however, public school officials merely have to show a legitimate educational excuse before suppressing student speech. . . .

Court Rulings Before *Hazelwood*

Case law prior to *Hazelwood* suggests that courts interpreted First Amendment rights for high school journalists in a broad sense. From *Tinker*[1] on, the courts upheld the rights of students to publish their newspapers without censorship. Though courts consistently protected First Amendment rights of students, many high school administrators continued to use their positions to intimidate students and advisers. Moreover, students often gave in to censorship either because they were unaware of their rights or unable to invest in legal resources. Also, school officials were often supported by school board members and community members who believed that high school students were too young—and too irresponsible—to examine controversial topics, like sex and drugs.

Prior to *Tinker*, [according to James L. Swanson and Christian L. Castle], "The Court (Supreme Court) did not initially acknowledge that students possessed rights. The Court instead supported parents' rights to educate their children as they wished." Throughout this century, the U.S. Supreme Court endorsed practices which would be considered extreme today. The Supreme Court did not render a significant decision in this area until the Warren Court opened the floodgates with *Tinker.* Thus, *Tinker* quickly became a landmark case, and subsequent cases—in lower courts as well as the Supreme Court—were decided on its legal theory.

In the 1990 *First Amendment Handbook,* James L. Swanson and Christian L. Castle state that "The evolving constitutional doctrine of students' expressive rights reveals a basic philosophical tension between two views of the school's role in education. The first view is that schools should indoctrinate

---

1. In the *Tinker v. Des Moines* decision, the Court ruled that students have the right to free expression, as long as such speech is not disruptive.

pupils by teaching majoritarian values and the limits of socially appropriate behavior with limited free expression. The second view is that schools should provide a forum for intellectual experimentation which mildly inculcates social values by encouraging free expression." When student newspapers are examined in the light of these competing values, it is not difficult to see why even well-intentioned school administrators seek to control content of school newspapers.

The *Hazelwood* Decision

Thus, although *Tinker* and subsequent decisions did much to encourage freedom of expression of high school students, there remained questions as to whether high school newspapers were public forums or whether they were actually a part of the curriculum and thus subject to school officials' control. Against this legal and philosophical backdrop the Supreme Court took up the case of three high school staff members on the "Spectrum," a student-produced newspaper at Hazelwood East High School in St. Louis, Missouri. . . .

In grappling with the role of public schools in society, federal and state courts often examine and weigh values, and the *Hazelwood* Court was no exception. The majority in *Hazelwood* supported Justice Hugo Black's dissent in *Tinker* that held that the degree of permissible school-imposed censorship of student expression varies with the student's age. The Court did not, however, give a clear line dividing "children" from "adults" and left open the question of whether children should be classified into subgroups by age for constitutional purposes.

The Court also resurrected a constitutional presumption, based on Black's dissent in *Tinker*, that high school administrators validly exercise their authority in supervising curricular activities. And finally, it determined that the school's role as publisher removes school-sponsored student media from the protected class of "public forums," thereby freeing school officials from the limitations of *Tinker*.

Censorship in California

In 1976 California state lawmakers passed a law intending to give high school journalism students greater protection from school-sponsored censorship. The law was challenged in a California federal appeals court just 16 days after *Hazelwood*. David Leeb served as editor of the school newspaper at Rancho Alamitos High School in southern California. He published an April Fool's Day spoof issue for which he wrote an article entitled "Nude Photos: Girls of Rancho." In the article, Leeb wrote that *Playboy* magazine planned to feature nude pictures of female Rancho students in an upcoming issue. Adjacent to the article was a picture purportedly showing five unnamed but identifiable Rancho female students lined up outside the school darkroom awaiting their turns to sign up for a photo session. The school's principal, James DeLong, was able to identify each student in the photo. DeLong then talked with the father of one of the girls pictured. The father, according to DeLong, expressed shock and outrage and threatened legal action. On April 2, DeLong stopped distribution of the paper. Leeb challenged the constitutionality of DeLong's action, charging prior restraint violated the California Constitution.

The Court of Appeals found that since California law gives greater constitutional protection to students than does the First Amendment, *Hazelwood* was inapplicable; only section 48907 and state court decisions control free expression questions involving California students. The court relied on an earlier case (*Bailey v. Loggins*), in which the California Supreme Court ruled content restrictions on state prison newspapers violate the State's Constitution. The *Bailey* Court had rejected the notion that the State acting as publisher of the prison newspaper, could exercise regulation as stringent as a private publisher. It also found that "the prison's regulations indicated an intent to open the papers as a limited public forum." In taking up the matter of Leeb, the Court of Appeals held that the school paper, like the one in *Bailey,* was a limited public forum. Therefore, no prior restraint could occur, unless a plaintiff would have a clear chance of prevailing in an action against the school. Aware that such a standard presents difficulties, however, the court offered further guidance by noting that to censor, schools should determine whether the publication would be likely to harm the reputation of another or hold that person up to shame, ridicule, or humiliation. By articulating a narrow standard, the court sought to avoid forcing schools into the "labyrinth of modern defamation law."

What makes Leeb interesting is that the facts are remarkably similar to those of *Hazelwood.* In both instances, students were not identified but were recognized by school administrators. Also, in both situations, the courts considered adoption of a tort liability standard for restricting speech. But although the *Hazelwood* majority rejected such a test, the Fourth District adopted one, acknowledging the liberal mandate of section 48907 and balancing student expression with the plaintiff's privacy rights. . . .

Broader Standards

California has created standards of interpretation of the First Amendment as applied to high school students which are broader and more protective than *Hazelwood.* California's standards permit restricting student expression only if the speech fits into specific categories. Libelous, slanderous, or obscene speech are prohibited. Also, material which incites students to break laws, disobey school rules or disrupt school activities may be restrained. The *Hazelwood* decision, however, permits suppression of student speech if the administrator's actions are supported by any reasonable educational purpose. In addition to defining what topics may be barred, the California standard flatly prohibits any prior restraint imposed to bar speech not otherwise proscribed by statute. *Hazelwood*, by contrast, allows prior restraint and any other regulation provided it serves a legitimate educational purpose.

The *Hazelwood* decision only stated the limits of First Amendment protections; it left open the possibility that states, like California, could create their own laws or regulations that provide journalists with greater protection. After *Hazelwood*, a total of 28 legislatures debated such laws, and five others besides California have passed them: Arkansas, Colorado, Iowa, Kansas and Massachusetts. Like California's section 48907, the laws in those states allow students to express themselves freely in school unless school officials can demonstrate it is libelous, obscene or will create a substantial disruption.

Though some states and courts have granted broader First Amendment rights to students, censorship of student expression, mainly in the form of publications, has only increased since *Hazelwood*. It appears, as Justice Brennan suggested, that *Hazelwood* has provided educators with much simpler means to legally stifle student discussion of topics deemed inappropriate for the high school setting. . . .

Alternatives to *Hazelwood*

The Commission of Inquiry into High School Journalism formed by the Robert F. Kennedy Memorial in the early 1970s saw the need for written guidelines to avoid disputes within high schools and costly litigation. Its members, moreover, hoped to improve the situation in high schools so that student journalists might become more responsible and develop a greater understanding and respect for the Constitution—and the First Amendment in particular.

The twenty-two members who made up the commission were respected, well-known citizens. They called for an end to unwarranted suppression of students' free speech rights. It appeared until *Hazelwood* that many federal and state courts were following the commission's findings on the negative impact of censorship in public schools. Since *Hazelwood*, however, the commission's conclusions about censorship appear all the more relevant today.

A number of courts have reviewed instances of administrative censorship and have examined specific school regulations on student expression; few courts have indicated precisely how guidelines should be constructed. The Fourth Circuit, however, did set out a detailed list of the attributes of constitutionally valid prior restraint guidelines in *Baughman v. Freienmuth*. Those guidelines are:

- Give precise criteria of what is to be forbidden so that a student will know what she can write;

- Provision for prompt approval and disapproval of what students submit;

- Specification of whether students may distribute material if administrators fail to act promptly; and

- An adequate and prompt appeal procedure.

Although a number of individuals as well as courts have suggested that any system of prior restraint is too restrictive, it would appear these guidelines have some advantages over the outcome of *Hazelwood*. They stipulate who may censor; they specify topics, words, or situations which could trigger censorship; and they provide for a method to settle differences—i.e., what can be done to change the offending article. Not only would written guidelines assist students and school officials, but they could also assist court interpretation of restrictions. Thus, it would be easier to determine whether the regulations are constitutional. . . .

A Continuing Struggle

California and a handful of other states have given students greater First Amendment protection than *Hazelwood*. Those states flatly prohibit censorship of student expression except in limited, statutorily defined areas. Until more states follow California's lead, student journalists—other than those in exceptional schools—will continue to struggle against school officials leery of allowing student publication of sensitive topics.

CHAPTER 3

Permitting Drug Tests for Student Athletes

Case Overview

Vernonia School District v. Acton (1995)

In the late 1980s the school district in the logging town of Vernonia, Oregon, recognized that drug use was becoming a growing problem among its students. After presentations and special classes failed to lessen the crisis, the Vernonia school district opted to implement a random drug testing program. Since student athletes were the leaders of the local drug culture, the policy targeted participants in interscholastic athletics. Any student who wanted to play sports was required to consent to the testing. All athletes took a drug test at the beginning of their sports season, and each week 10 percent of the athletes were randomly selected to take another drug test. Students who tested positive were given a second test; if that test also yielded proof of drug use, the student could either participate in a drug-treatment program or be suspended from his or her team for the remainder of the current season and the next athletic season.

The history of *Vernonia School District v. Acton* began in fall 1991, when seventh-grader James Acton, who wanted to play football for his grade school, and his parents refused to sign the testing consent form. After the school barred James from participating, he and his parents filed suit on the basis that the drug testing program violated the Fourth and Fourteenth Amendments. Their suit was dismissed by the district court, prompting an appeal. The U.S. Court of Appeals for the Ninth Circuit reversed the lower court's ruling, supporting the Actons' claim that their constitutional rights had been violated.

The school district took the next step by appealing the case to the Supreme Court. On June 26, 1995, in a decision written by Justice Antonin Scalia, the Court vacated the judgment and sent the case back to the Court of Appeals. According to Scalia, Vernonia's policy did not violate students' right to privacy because student athletes traditionally have little expectation of privacy, as evidenced by the fact that they shower and dress in locker rooms alongside their teammates. Furthermore, student athletes—all of whom participate voluntarily—are already held to higher standards than their peers, such as having to maintain a minimum grade point average and complying to rules established by their coaches. Later Court decisions have expanded on the ruling. For example, the 2002 decision *Board of Education of Independent School District No. 92 v. Earls* gave schools the right to require mandatory drug tests for students involved in all extracurricular activities, not just athletics.

> "By choosing to 'go out for the team,' [student athletes] voluntarily subject themselves to a degree of regulation even higher than that imposed on students generally."

The Court's Decision: Random Drug Tests of Student Athletes Is Constitutional

Antonin Scalia

The Vernonia School District's policy of requiring student athletes to submit to random drug tests does not violate the Fourth Amendment or students' right to privacy, the Supreme Court ruled in Vernonia School District v. Acton. *Justice Antonin Scalia, the author of the majority opinion, explains that students have traditionally been legally entitled to less privacy than adults. He further notes that student athletes have an even more reduced claim to privacy because they shower and change in locker rooms that lack privacy. Scalia concludes that the pervasive drug problem in the Vernonia school district and the necessity of protecting adolescents from the psychological and physical effects of substance abuse further justifies the tests, which do not violate the Fourth Amendment ban of unreasonable searches. Scalia has served on the Supreme Court since 1986.*

Petitioner Vernonia School District 47J (District) operates one high school and three grade schools in the logging community of Vernonia, Oregon. As elsewhere in small-town America, school sports play a prominent role in the town's life, and student athletes are admired in their schools and in the community.

Antonin Scalia, majority opinion, *Vernonia School District v. Acton,* June 26, 1995.

In 1995 the Supreme Court ruled that requiring student athletes to submit to random drug tests does not violate the Fourth Amendment or the students' right to privacy.
© David Madison/NewSport/CORBIS

A Growing Drug Problem

Drugs had not been a major problem in Vernonia schools. In the mid-to-late 1980's, however, teachers and administrators observed a sharp increase in drug use. Students began to speak out about their attraction to the drug culture, and to boast that there was nothing the school could do about it. Along with more drugs came more disciplinary problems. Between 1988 and 1989 the number of disciplinary referrals in Vernonia schools rose to more than twice the number reported in the early 1980's, and several students were suspended. Students became increasingly rude during class; outbursts of profane language became common.

Not only were student athletes included among the drug users but, as the District Court found, athletes were the leaders of the drug culture. This caused the District's administrators particular concern, since drug use increases the risk of sports-related injury. Expert testimony at the trial confirmed the deleterious effects of drugs on motivation, memory, judgment, reaction, coordination, and performance. The high school football and wrestling coach witnessed a severe sternum injury suffered by a wrestler, and various omissions of safety procedures and misexecutions by football players, all attributable in his belief to the effects of drug use.

Initially, the District responded to the drug problem by offering special classes, speakers, and presentations designed to deter drug use. It even brought in a specially trained dog to detect drugs, but the drug problem persisted. According to the District Court:

> [T]he administration was at its wits end and . . . a large segment of the student body, particularly those involved in interscholastic athletics, was in a state of rebellion. Disciplinary problems had reached "epidemic proportions." The coincidence of an almost three-fold increase in classroom disruptions and disciplinary reports along with the staff's direct observations of students using drugs or glamorizing drug and alcohol use led the administration to the inescapable conclusion that the rebellion was being fueled by alcohol and drug abuse as well as the student's misperceptions about the drug culture.

At that point, District officials began considering a drug-testing program. They held a parent "input night" to discuss the proposed Student Athlete Drug Policy (Policy), and the parents in attendance gave their unanimous approval. The school board approved the Policy for implementation in the fall of 1989. Its expressed purpose is to prevent student athletes from using drugs, to protect their health and safety, and to provide drug users with assistance programs.

How the Tests Work

The Policy applies to all students participating in interscholastic athletics. Students wishing to play sports must sign a form consenting to the testing and must obtain the written consent of their parents. Athletes are tested at the beginning of the season for their sport. In addition, once each week of the season the names of the athletes are placed in a "pool" from which a student, with the supervision of two adults, blindly draws the names of 10% of the athletes for random testing. Those selected are notified and tested that same day, if possible. . . .

If a sample tests positive, a second test is administered as soon as possible to confirm the result. If the second test is negative, no further action is taken. If the second test is positive, the athlete's parents are notified, and the school principal convenes a meeting with the student and his parents, at which the student is given the option of (1) participating for six weeks in an assistance program that includes weekly urinalysis, or (2) suffering suspension from athletics for the remainder of the current season and the next athletic season. The student is then retested prior to the start of the next athletic season for which he or she is eligible. The Policy states that a second offense results in automatic imposition of option (2); a third offense in suspension for the remainder of the current season and the next two athletic seasons.

The Rights of Children

In the fall of 1991, respondent James Acton, then a seventh-grader, signed up to play football at one of the District's grade schools. He was denied participation, however, because he and his parents refused to sign the testing consent forms. The Actons filed suit, seeking declaratory and injunctive relief from enforcement of the Policy on the grounds that it violated the Fourth and Fourteenth Amendments to the United States Constitution and Article I, 9, of the Oregon Constitution. After a bench trial, the District Court entered an order denying the claims on the merits and dismissing the action. The United States Court of Appeals for the Ninth Circuit reversed, holding that the Policy violated both the Fourth and Fourteenth Amendments and Article I, 9, of the Oregon Constitution. We granted certiorari. . . .

The first factor to be considered is the nature of the privacy interest upon which the search here at issue intrudes. The Fourth Amendment does not protect all subjective expectations of privacy, but only those that society recognizes as "legitimate." [*New Jersey v. T.L.O.* (1985)]. What expectations are legitimate varies, of course, with context. . . . Central, in our view, to the present case is the fact that the subjects of the Policy are (1) children, who (2) have been committed to the temporary custody of the State as schoolmaster.

Traditionally at common law, and still today, unemancipated minors lack some of the most fundamental rights of self-determination—including even the right of liberty in its narrow sense, i.e., the right to come and go at will. They are subject, even as to their physical freedom, to the control of their parents or guardians. When parents place minor children in private schools for their education, the teachers and administrators of those schools stand in loco parentis over the children entrusted to them. In fact, the tutor or schoolmaster is the very prototype of that status. As [eighteenth-century legal scholar William] Blackstone describes it, a parent "may . . . delegate part of his parental authority, during his life, to the tutor or schoolmaster of his child; who is then in loco parentis, and has such a portion of the power of the parent committed to his charge, viz. that of restraint and correction, as may be necessary to answer the purposes for which he is employed." . . .

A Lesser Expectation of Privacy

Fourth Amendment rights, no less than First and Fourteenth Amendment rights, are different in public schools than elsewhere; the "reasonableness" inquiry cannot disregard the schools' custodial and tutelary responsibility for children. For their own good and that of their classmates, public school children are routinely required to submit to various physical examinations, and to be vaccinated against various diseases.

According to the American Academy of Pediatrics, most public schools "provide vision and hearing screening and dental and dermatological checks. . . . Others also mandate scoliosis screening at appropriate grade levels." In the 1991–1992 school year, all 50 States required public-school students to be vaccinated against diphtheria, measles, rubella, and polio. Particularly with regard to medical examinations and procedures, therefore, "students within the school environment have a lesser expectation of privacy than members of the population generally." *T.L.O.* (Powell, J., concurring).

Legitimate privacy expectations are even less with regard to student athletes. School sports are not for the bashful. They require "suiting up" before each practice or event, and showering and changing afterwards. Public school locker rooms, the usual sites for these activities, are not notable for the privacy they afford. The locker rooms in Vernonia are typical: no individual dressing rooms are provided; shower heads are lined up along a wall, unseparated by any sort of partition or curtain; not even all the toilet stalls have doors. As the United States Court of Appeals for the Seventh Circuit has noted, there is "an element of 'communal undress' inherent in athletic participation," *Schaill by Kross v. Tippecanoe County School Corp.,* (1988).

There is an additional respect in which school athletes have a reduced expectation of privacy. By choosing to "go out for the team," they voluntarily subject themselves to a degree of regulation even higher than that imposed on students generally. In Vernonia's public schools, they must submit to a pre-season physical exam (James testified that his included the giving of a urine sample), they must acquire adequate insurance coverage or sign an insurance waiver, maintain a minimum grade point average, and comply with any "rules of conduct, dress, training hours and related matters as may be established for each sport by the head coach and athletic director with the principal's approval." Somewhat like adults who choose to participate in a "closely regulated industry," students who voluntarily participate in school athletics have reason to expect intrusions upon normal rights and privileges, including privacy. . . .

A Compelling Concern

Finally, we turn to consider the nature and immediacy of the governmental concern at issue here, and the efficacy of this means for meeting it. In both *Skinner* [*v. Railway Labor Executives Assn.* 1989] and [*Treasury Employees v.*] *Von Raab*, we characterized the government interest motivating the search as "compelling." *Skinner* (interest in preventing railway accidents); *Von Raab* (interest in insuring fitness of customs officials to interdict drugs and handle firearms). Relying on these cases, the District Court held that because the District's program also called for drug testing in the absence of individualized suspicion, the District "must demonstrate a 'compelling need' for the program." The Court of Appeals appears to have agreed with this view. It is a mistake, however, to think that the phrase "compelling state interest," in the Fourth Amendment context, describes a fixed, minimum quantum of governmental concern, so that one can dispose of a case by answering in isolation the question: Is there a compelling state interest here? Rather, the phrase describes an interest which appears important enough to justify the particular search at hand, in light of other factors which show the search to be relatively intrusive upon a genuine expectation of privacy. Whether that relatively high degree of government concern is necessary in this case or not, we think it is met.

That the nature of the concern is important—indeed, perhaps compelling can hardly be doubted. Deterring drug use by our Nation's schoolchildren is at least as important as enhancing efficient enforcement of the Nation's laws against the importation of drugs, which was the governmental concern in

Von Raab, or deterring drug use by engineers and trainmen, which was the governmental concern in *Skinner.* School years are the time when the physical, psychological, and addictive effects of drugs are most severe. [As stated by Richard A. Hanley,] "Maturing nervous systems are more critically impaired by intoxicants than mature ones are; childhood losses in learning are lifelong and profound"; "children grow chemically dependent more quickly than adults, and their record of recovery is depressingly poor." And of course the effects of a drug-infested school are visited not just upon the users, but upon the entire student body and faculty, as the educational process is disrupted. In the present case, moreover, the necessity for the State to act is magnified by the fact that this evil is being visited not just upon individuals at large, but upon children for whom it has undertaken a special responsibility of care and direction. Finally, it must not be lost sight of that this program is directed more narrowly to drug use by school athletes, where the risk of immediate physical harm to the drug user or those with whom he is playing his sport is particularly high. Apart from psychological effects, which include impairment of judgment, slow reaction time, and a lessening of the perception of pain, the particular drugs screened by the District's Policy have been demonstrated to pose substantial physical risks to athletes. . . .

A Constitutional Policy

Taking into account all the factors we have considered above—the decreased expectation of privacy, the relative unobtrusiveness of the search, and the severity of the need met by the search—we conclude Vernonia's Policy is reasonable and hence constitutional.

We caution against the assumption that suspicionless drug testing will readily pass constitutional muster in other contexts. The most significant element in this case is the first we discussed: that the Policy was undertaken in furtherance of the government's responsibilities, under a public school system, as guardian and tutor of children entrusted to its care. Just as when the government conducts a search in its capacity as employer (a warrantless search of an absent employee's desk to obtain an urgently needed file, for example), the relevant question is whether that intrusion upon privacy is one that a reasonable employer might engage in; so also when the government acts as guardian and tutor the relevant question is whether the search is one that a reasonable guardian and tutor might undertake. Given the findings of need made by the District Court, we conclude that in the present case it is.

We may note that the primary guardians of Vernonia's schoolchildren appear to agree. The record shows no objection to this districtwide program by any parents other than the couple before us here—even though, as we have described, a public meeting was held to obtain parents' views. We find insufficient basis to contradict the judgment of Vernonia's parents, its school board, and the District Court, as to what was reasonably in the interest of these children under the circumstances.

The Ninth Circuit held that Vernonia's Policy not only violated the Fourth Amendment, but also, by reason of that violation, contravened Article I . . . of the Oregon Constitution. Our conclusion that the former holding was in error means that the latter holding rested on a flawed premise. We therefore vacate the judgment, and remand the case to the Court of Appeals for further proceedings consistent with this opinion.

It is so ordered.

> "One searches today's majority opinion in vain for recognition that history and precedent establish that individualized suspicion is 'usually required' under the Fourth Amendment."

Dissenting Opinion: Drug Testing of Student Athletes Violates the Fourth Amendment

Sandra Day O'Connor

The random drug tests of student athletes implemented by the Vernonia School District cannot be justified because such tests do not meet the Fourth Amendment standard for reasonable searches, Sandra Day O'Connor writes in the following dissent of Vernonia School District v. Acton. She asserts that the policy of testing all student athletes is too broad and imprecise, adding that the Supreme Court has repeatedly ruled that mass, suspicionless searches are unconstitutional. According to O'Connor, Vernonia schools would be better served by testing students whose behavior is suspicious and indicative of drug use. O'Connor served on the Supreme Court from 1981 through 2006.

One searches today's majority opinion in vain for recognition that history and precedent establish that individualized suspicion is "usually required" under the Fourth Amendment (regardless of whether a warrant and probable cause are also required) and that, in the area of intrusive personal searches, the only recognized exception is for situations in

Sandra Day O'Connor, dissenting opinion, *Vernonia School District v. Acton,* June 26, 1995.

which a suspicion-based scheme would be likely ineffectual. Far from acknowledging anything special about individualized suspicion, the Court treats a suspicion-based regime as if it were just any run-of-the-mill, less intrusive alternative—that is, an alternative that officials may bypass if the lesser intrusion, in their reasonable estimation, is outweighed by policy concerns unrelated to practicability.

As an initial matter, I have serious doubts whether the Court is right that the District reasonably found that the lesser intrusion of a suspicion-based testing program outweighed its genuine concerns for the adversarial nature of such a program, and for its abuses. For one thing, there are significant safeguards against abuses. The fear that a suspicion-based regime will lead to the testing of "troublesome but not drug-likely" students, for example, ignores that the required level of suspicion in the school context is objectively reasonable suspicion. In this respect, the facts of our decision in *New Jersey v. T.L.O.* (1985), should be reassuring. There, we found reasonable suspicion to search a ninth-grade girl's purse for cigarettes after a teacher caught the girl smoking in the bathroom with a companion who admitted it. Moreover, any distress arising from what turns out to be a false accusation can be minimized by keeping the entire process confidential.

A Precedent for Suspicion-Based Testimony

For another thing, the District's concern for the adversarial nature of a suspicion-based regime (which appears to extend even to those who are rightly accused) seems to ignore the fact that such a regime would not exist in a vacuum. Schools already have adversarial, disciplinary schemes that require teachers and administrators in many areas besides drug use to investigate student wrongdoing (often by means of accusatory searches); to make determinations about whether the wrongdoing occurred; and to impose punishment. To such a scheme, suspicion-based drug testing would be only a minor addition.

The District's own elaborate disciplinary scheme is reflected in its handbook, which, among other things, lists the following disciplinary "problem areas" carrying serious sanctions: "DEFIANCE OF AUTHORITY," "DISORDERLY OR DISRUPTIVE CONDUCT INCLUDING FOUL LANGUAGE," "AUTOMOBILE USE OR MISUSE," "FORGERY OR LYING," "GAMBLING," "THEFT," "TOBACCO," "MISCHIEF," "VANDALISM," "RECKLESSLY ENDANGERING," "MENACING OR HARASSMENT," "ASSAULT," "FIGHTING," "WEAPONS," "EXTORTION," "EXPLOSIVE DEVICES," and "ARSON." . . .

("RESPONSIBILITIES OF SCHOOLS" include "To develop and distribute to parents and students reasonable rules and regulations governing student behavior and attendance" and "To provide fair and reasonable standards of conduct and to enforce those standards through appropriate disciplinary action.") The high number of disciplinary referrals in the record in this case illustrates the District's robust scheme in action.

In addition to overstating its concerns with a suspicion-based program, the District seems to have understated the extent to which such a program is less intrusive of students' privacy. By invading the privacy of a few students rather than many (nationwide, of thousands rather than millions), and by giving potential search targets substantial control over whether they will, in fact, be searched, a suspicion-based scheme is significantly less intrusive.

In any event, whether the Court is right that the District reasonably weighed the lesser intrusion of a suspicion-based scheme against its policy concerns is beside the point. As stated, a suspicion-based search regime is not just any less intrusive alternative; the individualized suspicion requirement has a legal pedigree as old as the Fourth Amendment itself, and it may not be easily cast aside in the name of policy concerns. It may only be forsaken, our cases in the personal search context have established, if a suspicion-based regime would likely be ineffectual.

An Effective Solution

But having misconstrued the fundamental role of the individualized suspicion requirement in Fourth Amendment analysis, the Court never seriously engages the practicality of such a requirement in the instant case. And that failure is crucial because nowhere is it less clear that an individualized suspicion requirement would be ineffectual than in the school context. In most schools, the entire pool of potential search targets—students—is under constant supervision by teachers and administrators and coaches, be it in classrooms, hallways, or locker rooms.

The record here indicates that the Vernonia schools are no exception. The great irony of this case is that most (though not all) of the evidence the District introduced to justify its suspicionless drug-testing program consisted of first- or second-hand stories of particular, identifiable students acting in ways that plainly gave rise to reasonable suspicion of in-school drug use—and thus that would have justified a drug-related search under our *T.L.O.* decision. . . . Small groups of students, for example, were observed by a teacher "passing joints back and forth" across the street at a restaurant before school and during school hours. Another group was caught skipping school and using drugs at one of the students' houses. Several students actually admitted their drug use to school officials (some of them being caught with marijuana pipes). One student presented himself to his teacher as "clearly obviously inebriated" and had to be sent home. Still another was observed dancing and singing at the top of his voice in the back of the classroom; when the teacher asked what was going on, he replied, "Well, I'm just high on life." To take a final example, on a certain road trip, the school wrestling coach smelled marijuana smoke in a hotel room occupied by four wrestlers, an observation that (after some questioning) would probably have given him reasonable suspicion to test one or all of them. . . .

In light of all this evidence of drug use by particular students, there is a substantial basis for concluding that a vigorous regime of suspicion-based testing (for which the District appears already to have rules in place) would have gone a long way toward solving Vernonia's school drug problem while preserving the Fourth Amendment rights of James Acton and others like him. And were there any doubt about such a conclusion, it is removed by indications in the record that suspicion-based testing could have been supplemented by an equally vigorous campaign to have Vernonia's parents encourage their children to submit to the District's voluntary drug testing program. In these circumstances, the Fourth Amendment dictates that a mass, suspicionless search regime is categorically unreasonable.

Individualized Suspicion Requirement Applies to Students

I recognize that a suspicion-based scheme, even where reasonably effective in controlling in-school drug use, may not be as effective as a mass, suspicionless testing regime. In one sense, that is obviously true just as it is obviously true that suspicion-based law enforcement is not as effective as mass, suspicionless enforcement might be. "But there is nothing new in the realization" that Fourth Amendment protections come with a price. *Arizona v. Hicks* (1987). Indeed, the price we pay is higher in the criminal context, given that police do not closely observe the entire class of potential search targets (all citizens in the area) and must ordinarily adhere to the rigid requirements of a warrant and probable cause.

The principal counterargument to all this, central to the Court's opinion, is that the Fourth Amendment is more lenient with respect to school searches. That is no doubt correct, for, as the Court explains, schools have traditionally had special guardian-like responsibilities for children that necessitate a degree of constitutional leeway. This principle explains the considerable Fourth Amendment leeway we gave school officials in *T.L.O.* In that case, we held that children at school do not enjoy two of the Fourth Amendment's categorical protections against unreasonable searches and seizures: the warrant requirement and the probable cause requirement. And this was true even though the same children enjoy such protections "in a nonschool setting." (Powell, J., concurring).

The instant case, however, asks whether the Fourth Amendment is even more lenient than that, i.e., whether it is so lenient that students may be deprived of the Fourth Amendment's only remaining, and most basic, categorical protection: its strong preference for an individualized suspicion requirement, with its accompanying antipathy toward personally intrusive, blanket searches of mostly innocent people. It is not at all clear that people in prison lack this categorical protection, and we have said "we are not yet ready to hold that the schools and the prisons need be equated for purposes of the Fourth Amendment." *T.L.O.* Thus, if we are to mean what we often proclaim—that students do not "shed their constitutional rights . . . at the schoolhouse gate," *Tinker v. Des Moines Independent Community School Dist.,* (1969)— the answer must plainly be no. . . .

Random Tests Are Not the Answer

Intrusive, blanket searches of school children, most of whom are innocent, for evidence of serious wrongdoing are not part of any traditional school function of which I am aware. Indeed, many schools, like many parents, prefer to trust their children unless given reason to do otherwise. As James Acton's father said on the witness stand, "[suspicionless testing] sends a message to children that are trying to be responsible citizens

... that they have to prove that they're innocent ... , and I think that kind of sets a bad tone for citizenship."

I find unpersuasive the Court's reliance on the widespread practice of physical examinations and vaccinations, which are both blanket searches of a sort. Of course, for these practices to have any Fourth Amendment significance, the Court has to assume that these physical exams and vaccinations are typically "required" to a similar extent that urine testing and collection is required in the instant case, i.e., that they are required regardless of parental objection and that some meaningful sanction attaches to the failure to submit. In any event, without forming any particular view of such searches, it is worth noting that a suspicion requirement for vaccinations is not merely impractical; it is nonsensical, for vaccinations are not searches for anything in particular and so there is nothing about which to be suspicious. Nor is this saying anything new; it is the same theory on which, in part, we have repeatedly upheld certain inventory searches. As for physical examinations, the practicability of a suspicion requirement is highly doubtful because the conditions for which these physical exams ordinarily search, such as latent heart conditions, do not manifest themselves in observable behavior the way school drug use does.

It might also be noted that physical exams (and of course vaccinations) are not searches for conditions that reflect wrongdoing on the part of the student, and so are wholly nonaccusatory and have no consequences that can be regarded as punitive. These facts may explain the absence of Fourth Amendment challenges to such searches. By contrast, although I agree with the Court that the accusatory nature of the District's testing program is diluted by making it a blanket one, any testing program that searches for conditions plainly reflecting serious wrongdoing can never be made wholly nonaccusatory from the student's perspective, the motives for the program notwithstanding; and for the same reason, the substantial consequences that can flow from a positive test, such as suspension from sports, are invariably—and quite reasonably—understood as punishment. The best proof that the District's testing program is to some extent accusatory can be found in James Acton's own explanation on the witness stand as to why he did not want to submit to drug testing: "Because I feel that they have no reason to think I was taking drugs." It is hard to think of a manner of explanation that resonates more intensely in our Fourth Amendment tradition than this. . . .

It cannot be too often stated that the greatest threats to our constitutional freedoms come in times of crisis. But we must also stay mindful that not all government responses to such times are hysterical overreactions; some crises are quite real, and when they are, they serve precisely as the compelling state interest that we have said may justify a measured intrusion on constitutional rights. The only way for judges to mediate these conflicting impulses is to do what they should do anyway: stay close to the record in each case that appears before them, and make their judgments based on that alone. Having reviewed the record here, I cannot avoid the conclusion that the District's suspicionless policy of testing all student-athletes sweeps too broadly, and too imprecisely, to be reasonable under the Fourth Amendment.

| *"Unemancipated minors do not enjoy all the rights of adults."*

Vernonia Is a Fair Response to the Problem of Drugs in Schools

George Will

In June 1995, in the case of Vernonia School District v. Acton, *the Supreme Court ruled that student athletes voluntarily give up their right to privacy and therefore cannot refuse to consent to a random drug testing program. George Will contends in the following selection that the court was right to support the constitutionality of such tests. He argues that the drug problem experienced in the Vernonia, Oregon, school district is a serious epidemic that cannot be stemmed by restricting tests to students who are disruptive or behave suspiciously. Will is a syndicated columnist.*

The question before the Supreme Court was whether an appellate judge was correct when he said, "Children are compelled to attend school but nothing suggests that they lose their right to privacy in their excretory functions when they do so." By a 6-3 vote the Court decided [in June 1995] that the public school athletes voluntarily compromise that right in Vernonia, Ore.

A Reasonable Search

In the late 1980s Vernonia teachers and administrators became alarmed by a boastful, flaunting embrace of drugs by students who became increasingly rude, profane and disruptive. Authorities noted that athletes, who often loom large in the lives of small towns, were leaders of the drug culture. And authorities worried about drug use increasing the risk of sports injuries. In addition to psychological effects on motivation, drugs can impair judgment, slow reaction time, mask pain, interfere with the body's normal fatigue responses, and increase heart rate and blood pressure. So the school district instituted a policy of random urinalysis drug testing of all athletes. But James Acton, then a seventh-grader eager to play football, objected, arguing that the testing violates the Constitution's Fourth Amendment protection against "unreasonable searches."

So, what is "reasonable"? Vernonia's policy is, says the Court. Speaking through Justice [Antonin] Scalia, whose opinion was joined by Justices [William] Rehnquist, [Anthony] Kennedy, [Ruth Bader] Ginsburg, [Clarence] Thomas, and [Stephen] Breyer, the Court noted that it is settled law that such testing constitutes a search. Reasonableness is judged by balancing the intrusiveness of a search against the promotion of a legitimate governmental interest, which the prevention of drug use by children surely is.

Unemancipated minors do not enjoy all the rights of adults, particularly in the context of a school acting somewhat in loco parentis, charged with inculcating civility. Students are routinely required to have vaccinations and physical examinations. And regarding non-compulsory participation in athletics, Scalia says: "School sports are not for the bashful." Athletes commonly submit to regulations and codes of conduct. So, "We find insufficient basis to contradict the judgment of Vernonia's parents, its school board, and the district court, as to what was reasonably in the interest of these children under the circumstances."

Ignoring the Drug Problem

Justice [Sandra Day] O'Connor, dissenting and joined by Justices [John Paul] Stevens and [David] Souter (appointees of

[Ronald] Reagan, [Gerald] Ford and [George H.W.] Bush, respectively), says the record in this case does not demonstrate that there was a drug problem at Acton's particular school. So much for trusting the judgment of the community and its institutions. O'Connor says that Fourth Amendment law generally forbids broad "searches" of whole groups (in this case, athletes). Individualized suspicion is required to justify searches. She quotes a 1925 Supreme Court ruling: "It would be intolerable and unreasonable if a prohibition agent were authorized to stop every automobile on the chance of finding liquor and thus subject all persons lawfully using the highways to the inconvenience and indignity of such a search."

But adult drivers have different rights than students, especially the subcategory of voluntary student athletes. Furthermore, O'Connor concedes that the record "demonstrates there was a drug-related discipline problem in Vernonia of 'epidemic proportions.'" The *Oxford English Dictionary* defines "epidemic" as "widely prevalent, universal." So what is wrong with a testing program that targets a category of persons—athletes—most identified with something "widely prevalent," persons who can avoid testing by avoiding non-compulsory athletic activity?

O'Connor would have the district deal with its drug problem, which she says the record showed to be "of epidemic proportions" (epidemic, but not proven to have touched Acton's school?), by focusing testing on students whose behavior is disruptive or otherwise suspicious. She says breezily that "any distress arising from what turns out to be a false accusation can be minimized by keeping the entire process confidential."

What America is she living in? The real America is full of people as litigious as Acton, people encouraged by court rulings to be exquisitely sensitive about their rights and dismissive of the judgments of local authorities. In this America, false accusations breed lawsuits, so O'Connor's suggestion is a recipe for causing the district to back off and live with its epidemic.

Time was when the discipline problems in American schools concerned running in the halls and cutting classes. But Vernonia is in today's America, where rights are trumps and seventh-graders get lawyers and local authorities get no respect. Which just may have something to do with the fact that the Vernonia school district, which is not unlike thousands of others, has a handbook in which the list of disciplinary "problem areas" includes "recklessly endangering," "weapons," "extortion," "arson" and "explosive devices."

"Unless and until a school district can show that it has a genuine problem, the Fourth Amendment should prevent the district from requiring random testing."

Random Drug Tests Violate Students' Right to Privacy

Benjamin Dowling-Sendor

The Supreme Court's ruling in Vernonia School District v. Acton, *which upheld the constitutionality of random drug tests for public school athletes, has led to further attempts by school districts to implement tests for students participating in a variety of extracurricular activities. In the following selection Benjamin Dowling-Sendor criticizes the ruling made by the Eighth U.S. Circuit Court of Appeals in* Miller v. Wilkes. *He contends that the decision, which supported a Cave City, Arkansas, school district's drug testing policy, is an indication that Vernonia has resulted in students' gradually losing more and more of their rights to privacy. According to Dowling-Sendor, while Vernonia schools had a serious drug problem, such an epidemic did not exist in Cave City, Arkansas. Furthermore, because the Cave City policy required students who wished to participate in any extracurricular activity to consent to random drug tests—not just athletes who might suffer serious injuries due to drug abuse— such a policy could not be justified under the Vernonia precedent. Dowling-Sendor concludes that the Fourth Amendment should guard against random drug testing unless a school district can prove its schools have a significant drug problem. Dowling-Sendor is an assistant appellate defender of North Carolina in Durham.*

Benjamin Dowling-Sendor, "The Drug-Testing Dilemma," *American School Board Journal*, October 1999. Copyright © 1999 by the National School Boards Association. All rights reserved. Reproduced by permission of the author.

Lawyers like to scare people with "slippery slope" arguments, warning us that giving someone the right or power to engage in particular conduct will inevitably lead to extensions of that power. In other words, once a court makes a decision in one case that sends the law down a certain path, another court in another case might send it further down that path, but without the reasons that justified the first decision— or, give them an inch and they'll take a mile. As shown by the [March 1999] decision of the 8th U.S. Circuit Court of Appeals in *Miller ex rel. Miller v. Wilkes,* legal support for random, suspicionless drug testing of students seems to be just such a slippery-slope phenomenon.

Drug Testing in Arkansas

Here are the facts, as reported in the 8th Circuit's opinion: The Cave City, Ark., school board adopted a policy of random testing of urine samples for students in grades seven through 12 as a condition of participating in any extracurricular activity, starting with the 1997–98 school year. The test screens for illegal drugs (including improperly used prescription drugs) and alcohol.

The policy requires each student and the student's parent or guardian to sign a form consenting to random testing. If the student or parent refuses to give written consent to the testing, or if a student refuses to be tested when randomly selected, the student is barred from taking part in any extracurricular activities. A positive test results in 20 days of probation; also, the school will notify the parent or guardian about the result and will recommend counseling or rehabilitation. A student who tests positive will be retested after 21 days, and the student will be banned from extracurricular activities for a year if the second test is positive. Such a student can participate in extracurricular activities after a year if the student tests negative at that time. The superintendent's office keeps test results in a separate file and destroys a student's test files after graduation or two years after the student leaves the Cave City schools.

Resisting the Policy

A student named Pathe Miller wanted to participate in several extracurricular activities, such as the radio club, prom committees, a quiz bowl, and school dances. But when Pathe and his father, Troy Miller, refused to give written consent to the random testing, the school district barred Pathe from taking part in any extracurricular activities. Pathe and his father sued the school board and the superintendent in federal district court, contending that the testing policy violated the Fourth Amendment's prohibition against unreasonable searches and seizures.

When the district court ruled in favor of the school board and superintendent, Pathe and his father appealed to the 8th Circuit. In a unanimous decision, the 8th Circuit affirmed the district court's ruling.

Relying on *Vernonia*

In the court's decision, Judge Pasco M. Bowman II noted that urinalysis comes within the Fourth Amendment's protection against unreasonable searches and seizures. Judge Bowman also acknowledged that the Cave City testing program was random and that students were selected for testing without a warrant, probable cause, or even individualized suspicion of wrongdoing. But he observed that in some cases not directly related to law enforcement, a warrant, probable cause, and individualized suspicion are not necessary if a government agency has a special need to discover hazardous conditions or to prevent a hazardous condition from developing. In such cases, Bowman stated, the Fourth Amendment requires courts to weigh the legitimate expectation of privacy and the nature of the proposed government intrusion against the nature and urgency of the government's interest and the efficacy of the proposed search in serving that interest.

To balance those interests in this case, Judge Bowman looked for guidance to the Supreme Court's 1995 decision in *Vernonia School District 47J v. Acton,* which upheld a urinalysis program that made testing a condition of participation in extracurricular school athletic programs. The high court emphasized that the school board in Vernonia, Ore., had adopted the testing program because of an increase in student drug use, an increase in disciplinary problems, and a finding that student athletes were "'the leaders of the drug culture'" in the Vernonia schools.

Noting the special health dangers that drugs pose for athletes, the Supreme Court also emphasized the substantial measures the district used to protect the privacy and testing results of students, the fact that expectations of privacy are reduced in the public school setting, and the fact that student athletes—who dress and undress together in locker rooms—have even less legitimate expectation of bodily privacy. The Supreme Court also found that random drug testing of student athletes would be more effective, or at least as effective, as testing based on reasonable, individualized suspicion of drug use by a particular student.

In her concurring opinion in *Vernonia,* Justice Ruth Bader Ginsburg was alert to the slippery-slope dangers the ruling posed. She emphasized that special factors peculiar to student athletes justified the testing program in Vernonia, and she stressed that the Supreme Court's ruling did not necessarily extend to random testing of all students.

School District Versus Students

In the *Miller* case, Judge Bowman observed, students have a reduced expectation of privacy, as the Supreme Court had found in *Vernonia.* The high court's finding that student athletes have even less legitimate expectations of privacy than other students did not sway him. In Bowman's view, "simply being a student in a public school is '[c]entral' to a lowered expectation of privacy." Bowman then added that even non-athletic extracurricular activities lower the legitimate privacy expectations of participating students. Noting that such activities have rules that are enforced by school employees, he concluded that "students who elect to be involved in school activities have a legitimate expectation of privacy that is diminished to a level below that of the already lowered expectation of non-participating students." Judge Bowman also found that the Cave City School District's policy protected students' privacy as least as well as the policy upheld by the Supreme Court in *Vernonia*. For example, the test screened only for drugs and alcohol, the results were reported only to the superintendent or an employee designated by the superintendent, and a positive test did not result in reports to law enforcement agencies or suspension or expulsion.

Judge Bowman then examined the strength of the school district's interests. Bowman stated that substance abuse is a serious problem in the nation's schools. He admitted that in contrast to the evidence in *Vernonia*, which showed a serious substance abuse problem in the Vernonia schools, the evidence in this case did not show a crisis in the Cave City schools. But once again, Bowman concluded that the distinction between this case and *Vernonia* did not tip the balance against the testing program. He reasoned that the Cave City schools had a sufficiently strong interest in preventing the rise of a serious substance abuse problem to justify the program. "We see no reason that a school district should be compelled to wait until there is a demonstrable problem with substance abuse among its own students before the district is constitutionally permitted to take measures that will help protect its schools against the sort of 'rebellion' proven in *Vernonia* . . . ," he wrote.

Balancing the interests of students and the school district, Judge Bowman concluded that the school district's interest in preventing possible abuse is "important enough" to justify the random testing program.

An Intrusion on Privacy

Substance abuse is a serious problem in American schools, and I have no doubt that it occurs in the schools of Cave City as well as in the schools of New York City. But, as a matter of legal reasoning, I fear that Judge Bowman and his colleagues on the 8th Circuit have taken us far down the slippery slope. As I read it, four facts were important to the Supreme Court's decision in *Vernonia:* (1) The legitimate expectation of privacy among students in public school is less than the legitimate expectation of other citizens in other settings; (2) student athletes have an even lower legitimate expectation of privacy; (3) drugs are especially dangerous to athletes; and (4) the Vernonia schools were suffering from a proven substance-abuse crisis, especially among student athletes. Only one of those four facts applies in *Miller:* the generally reduced expectation of privacy of students. Judge Bowman's argument that extracurricular activities generally require intrusion into privacy is not persuasive. Surely members of the radio club do not have the same low expectation of privacy as members of the football team, who dress and undress together in locker rooms. Surely the members of the radio club do not risk physical injury from substance abuse as football players do. And while I agree that school districts have a genuine interest in preventing the rise of substance abuse, it is a speculative interest that does not measure up to the demonstrated crisis in *Vernonia* and that should not trump the privacy interests of students.

In my view, the key factor in deciding whether to adopt a policy of random drug testing should be whether there is evidence of a substance-abuse problem in the district's schools. Random urinalysis—even when there are measures designed to minimize the intrusion into students' privacy—is a substantial interference with privacy. The general lament that substance abuse is a major problem in the nation should not be sufficient to justify a testing program in a particular school district.

Unless and until a school district can show that it has a genuine problem, the Fourth Amendment should prevent the district from requiring random testing. If a district can show that it has a real substance abuse problem, however, I believe that *Vernonia* would permit it to adopt a random testing program reasonably tailored to the scope of the problem.

| "Few, if any, published data support the
effectiveness of student drug testing."

Schools Should Seek Alternatives to Random Drug Tests

Oscar G. Bukstein

In 1995 the Supreme Court ruled in the case Vernonia School District v. Acton *that schools can require student athletes to submit to random drug tests. In the following viewpoint Oscar G. Bukstein asserts that although drug tests have helped reduce substance abuse in the workplace and military, student drug testing has not been proven effective and thus should not be too readily implemented by school districts. Rather, he argues that if schools are concerned about drug use, they should focus on a broader treatment program that features not only drug testing but also prevention and treatment programs. Bukstein also contends that if drug testing is to be performed, it should focus not on athletes, who are the lowest-risk youth for substance abuse, but rather on students whose behavioral and emotional problems are an indication of drug use. Bukstein is an associate professor of psychiatry at the University of Pittsburgh School of Medicine.*

Despite hundreds of millions of dollars of federal, state, local, and private funds spent to support drug-prevention programs, drug use among high school, and even middle school, students remains high. Often in desperation, secondary schools have turned to random drug testing as a potential aid in preventing illicit substance use or use disorders. "Ran

Oscar G. Bukstein, "Drug Testing in Schools: Good Practice or Good Politics? Random Drug Testing of Adolescent Students Sounds Like Good Commonsense Policy—but Where's the Evidence?" *Behavioral Health Management,* vol. 24, July/August 2004, p. 17. Copyright © 2004 by Medquest Communications, LLC. Reproduced by permission.

dom drug testing," in this context, is distinguished from school policies that require drug testing "for cause" or suspicion of use. Schools have used for-cause drug testing for years and usually follow carefully delineated procedures, often including parental consent. Random drug testing has been the subject of recent court decisions and is controversial.

Although the Supreme Court has ruled that the random testing of all students is unconstitutional, the Court recently held in a five-to-four decision that a mandatory drug-testing program for students involved in extracurricular activities is permissible (*Board of Education of Independent School District No. 92 of Pottawatomie County v. Earls* [2002]). The Court previously had ruled that student athletes could be tested (*Vernonia School District 47J v. Acton* [1995]). These decisions greatly expand the potential for school drug testing.

Drug Testing Students Is Not Effective

Earlier [in 2004], the Bush administration proposed to add $23 million to support school drug-testing programs. In fiscal year 2003, the Department of Education's Office of Safe and Drug-Free Schools awarded several million dollars in grants to schools around the country for demonstration projects of student drug-testing programs. Despite the concerns of some civil libertarians and the limitation of testing to students participating in extracurricular activities, much enthusiasm exists for implementing and expanding drug testing in many public and private schools.

Unfortunately, little science and few data support the enthusiasm. While drug-testing programs have had some effect in decreasing drug use in the workplace and the military, few, if any, published data support the effectiveness of student drug testing, although John Walters, director of the White House Office of National Drug Control Policy (ONDCP), has stated that "testing has been shown to be extremely effective at reducing drug use in schools and businesses all over the country." Because until recently the constitutionality of random drug testing was uncertain, there has been little time to implement studies of its effectiveness. Now there is an assumption that random drug testing works. Before we either provide wholesale support for or condemnation of student drug testing, we should know the limited evidence for and against it, as well as consider the general pros and cons of this practice.

Results of Studies

As part of the *Monitoring the Future* study, [Ryoko] Yamaguchi et al. provided descriptive information on the drug testing conducted by schools participating in the study. Drug testing in these programs was not associated with the prevalence of self-reported illicit drug use or with the rate among experienced marijuana users. The investigators reported identical rates of drug use in schools with and without drug-testing policies, including random testing policies. Proponents of drug testing assert that the study's methodology was flawed, but the study, in fact, represents one of the best examples of science in this area, short of a randomized intervention trial.

[L.] Goldberg and associates compared two high schools, one with a policy of mandatory drug testing prior to sports participation and a control high school with no such policy. Although the high schools differed somewhat along racial/ethnic lines, self-report from athletes at the school with drug testing found lower 30-day illicit drug use and athletic-enhancing drug use than those from the control high school. Unfortunately, many risk factors associated with drug use—including norms of use, belief in lower risk of drugs, and poorer attitudes toward school—increased more among the student athletes at the school with drug testing than at the school without drug testing.

The remaining "evidence" for the effectiveness of random drug testing includes anecdotes and unpublished surveys. Moreover, in the one study (above) suggestive of a positive relationship between drug testing and decreased substance use, the authors expressed caution regarding the results and advised that larger studies, extending over several years, would have to be completed before student drug testing was supported by empirical evidence.

Only One Component

ONDCP suggests that schools tread carefully before implementing drug-testing policies or programs, advising school administrators to seek the advice and input of attorneys, parents, and teachers, as well as prevention and treatment professionals. Also recommended are policies that are not punitive but rather focus upon positive test results (confirmed by a second drug test) and mandate further evaluation and/or treatment. Expulsions or suspensions, says ONDCP, should be delivered only in cases of noncompliance with evaluation or treatment. Furthermore, drug testing should be only one component of a broader program, including prevention and treatment elements, designed to reduce student drug use. Clearly, drug testing has potential benefits, including reduced adolescent drug use and early identification for intervention. However, obstacles remain. At the moment, random drug testing is approved only for youth involved in athletics and other extracurricular activities, although these adolescents represent the lowest-risk youth for drug use and associated problems; thus, adolescents at highest risk will not be tested. Furthermore, drug testing does not yet include alcohol, still the most common "drug" of abuse. Risks of a random testing program include invasion of privacy with or without parental permission; costs of the program in terms of time, money, and other resources; potential violations of confidentiality; and creating a more adversarial environment between students and school staff. Although the ONDCP recommends development of procedures for referral to professionals for evaluation and possible treatment, schools cannot ensure that students who do not have health insurance will be able to access appropriate services or that those with health insurance will have access to benefits and providers offering what they need. In this era of decreasing budgets, resources that go to drug testing ($10 to 30 per test) may come at the expense of other resources, such as counselors and prevention programs, which research has shown to be highly effective.

Focus on Evidence-Based Practices

Because we can test students does not mean that we should. From the federal government to professional societies, evidence-based practices are supported for both education and behavioral medicine, and random student drug testing without cause does not yet have evidence-based support. Therefore, prior to advocating widespread support or adoption of such drug-testing policies, federal and local governments should support rigorous controlled studies of student drug testing. Only when evidence of positive effects for student drug testing becomes available should adoption and funding of random drug-testing programs by governments and school districts be considered.

In the meantime, we should be supporting a more considered form of student drug testing—that for "cause or suspicion." Youth with drug problems almost always manifest a range of behavioral and emotional problems that are obvious to school staff, parents, and peers. Although this represents a distinct minority of high school students, these are the students who need to be tested and would be most helped by subsequent intervention. All students, particularly high-risk students, potentially could benefit from this approach to testing. Beyond this, government and school districts should continue to focus on evidence-based practices rather than politically expedient ones.

CHAPTER 4

The Pledge of Allegiance and the First Amendment

Case Overview

Michael A. Newdow v. U.S. Congress et al. (2002)

American students have been reciting the Pledge of Allegiance for more than a century. The original pledge read: "I pledge allegiance to my Flag and the Republic for which it stands: one Nation indivisible, with Liberty and Justice for all." The pledge was altered slightly on two occasions, most notably in 1954, when the phrase "under God" was added by Congress. The presence of a religious reference in a pledge made by public school children has raised questions of whether the Pledge of Allegiance violates the Establishment Clause—the line in the First Amendment that states, "Congress shall make no law respecting an establishment of religion."

In March 2000 Michael Newdow, an atheist and divorced father whose daughter attended school in the Elk Grove Unified School District in California, brought this issue to the federal courts. He contended that the words "under God" violated the Establishment Clause and asked that the Pledge of Allegiance no longer be recited daily. After the U.S. District Court for the Eastern District of California dismissed Newdow's complaint, he appealed to the U.S. Court of Appeals for the Ninth Circuit. On June 26, 2002, in the case *Michael A. Newdow v. U.S. Congress et al.*, the appellate court ruled in favor of Newdow. In his ruling Judge Alfred T. Goodwin argued that Supreme Court precedent shows that the Pledge of Allegiance, as presently written, runs counter to the Establishment Clause. Goodwin also asserted that schools do not have the right to coerce children into reciting the pledge.

The school district appealed the case to the Supreme Court. In June 2004 the high court reversed the earlier decision, but not by addressing the constitutional issues. Rather, the decision by John Paul Stevens explained that Newdow lacked the standing to sue on behalf of his daughter because the girl's mother had sole legal custody of her and therefore the right to determine how she was educated. Consequently, the debate over whether reciting the Pledge of Allegiance infringes on the right of students to be free of religious indoctrination remains unsettled.

"We may assume arguendo *that public officials do not unconstitutionally endorse religion when they recite the Pledge, yet it does not follow that schools may coerce impressionable young schoolchildren to recite it."*

The Court's Decision: The Pledge of Allegiance Violates the First Amendment

Alfred T. Goodwin

In 2002 the U.S. Court of Appeals for the Ninth Circuit considered a case submitted by Michael Newdow, an atheist who charged that the daily recitation of the Pledge of Allegiance at the public school his daughter attended was unconstitutional because the pledge contains the phrase "under God." The court ruled in Newdow's favor. In his opinion, excerpted here, Judge Alfred T. Goodwin argues that Supreme Court rulings in school prayer cases set a precedent for the conclusion that the policy of the Elk Grove Unified School District coerces students into performing a religious act and is thus unconstitutional. According to Goodwin, the inclusion of "under God" means that the pledge violates the Establishment Clause of the First Amendment, which bars the establishment of religion in the public sphere. Goodwin is a judge on the U.S. Court of Appeals for the Ninth Circuit, which covers the western United States, Alaska, and Hawaii.

Michael Newdow appeals pro se [without an attorney] a judgment dismissing his challenge to the constitutionality of the words "under God" in the Pledge of Allegiance to the Flag. Newdow argues that the addition of these words by a

Alfred T. Goodwin, opinion, *Michael A. Newdow v. U.S. Congress et al.,* June 26, 2002.

1954 federal statute to the previous version of the Pledge of Allegiance (which made no reference to God) and the daily recitation in the classroom of the Pledge of Allegiance, with the added words included, by his daughter's public school teacher are violations of the Establishment Clause of the First Amendment to the United States Constitution. . . .

Newdow's Claim

Newdow does not allege that his daughter's teacher or school district requires his daughter to participate in reciting the Pledge. Rather, he claims that his daughter is injured when she is compelled to "watch and listen as her state-employed teacher in her state-run school leads her classmates in a ritual proclaiming that there is a God, and that our's [sic] is 'one nation under God.'"

Newdow's complaint in the district court challenged the constitutionality, under the First Amendment, of the 1954 Act, the California statute,[1] and the school district's policy requiring teachers to lead willing students in recitation of the Pledge. He sought declaratory and injunctive relief, but did not seek damages.

The school districts and their superintendents (collectively, "school district defendants") filed a Federal Rule of Civil Procedure 12(b)(6) motion to dismiss for failure to state a claim. Magistrate Judge Peter A. Nowinski held a hearing at which the school district defendants requested that the court rule only on the constitutionality of the Pledge, and defer any ruling on sovereign immunity. The United States Congress, the United States, and the President of the United States (collectively, "the federal defendants") joined in the motion to dismiss filed by the school district defendants. The magistrate judge reported findings and a recommendation that the district court hold that the daily Pledge ceremony in the schools

1. requiring public schools to begin the day with the Pledge of Allegiance or other patriotic exercises

A member of the American Atheists holds up signs during a protest outside the Ninth Circuit Court of Appeals in San Francisco. In 2002 the court ruled that the Pledge of Allegiance violates the Establishment Clause of the First Amendment. Justin Sullivan/ Getty Images

did not violate the Establishment Clause. District Judge Edward J. Schwartz approved the recommendation and entered a 4 judgment of dismissal. This appeal followed. . . .

Newdow's Standing

Article III standing is a jurisdictional issue. Accordingly, it "may be raised at any stage of the proceedings, including for the first time on appeal." *See A-Z Intern. v. Phillip* (9th Cir. 1999). To satisfy standing requirements, a plaintiff must prove that "(1) it has suffered an 'injury in fact' that is (a) concrete and particularized and (b) actual or imminent, not conjectural or hypothetical; (2) the injury is fairly traceable to the challenged action of the defendant; and (3) it is likely, as opposed to merely speculative, that the injury will be redressed by a favorable decision." *Friends of the Earth, Inc. v. Laidlaw Envtl. Servs. (TOC), Inc.* (2000) (citing *Lujan v. Defenders of Wildlife* (1992)).

Newdow has standing as a parent to challenge a practice that interferes with his right to direct the religious education of his daughter. "Parents have a right to direct the religious upbringing of their children and, on that basis, have standing to protect their right." *Doe v. Madison Sch. Dist. No. 321* (9th Cir. 1999).

Newdow has standing to challenge the EGUSD's [Elk Grove Unified School District] policy and practice regarding the recitation of the Pledge because his daughter is currently enrolled in elementary school in the EGUSD. However, Newdow has no standing to challenge the SCUSD's [Sacramento City Unified School District] policy and practice because his daughter is not currently a student there. The SCUSD and its superintendent have not caused Newdow or his daughter an "injury in fact" that is "actual or imminent, not conjectural or hypothetical." *Laidlaw* (citing *Lujan*, 504 U.S. at 560–561).

The Establishment Clause

[1] The Establishment Clause of the First Amendment states that "Congress shall make no law respecting an establishment of religion," a provision that "the Fourteenth Amendment makes applicable with full force to the States and their school districts." *Lee v. Weisman* (1992). Over the last three decades, the Supreme Court has used three interrelated tests to analyze alleged violations of the Establishment Clause in the realm of public education: the three-prong test set forth in *Lemon v. Kurtzman* (1971); the "endorsement" test, first articulated by Justice [Sandra Day] O'Connor in her concurring opinion in *Lynch v. Donnelly* (1984), and later adopted by a majority of the Court in *County of Allegheny v. ACLU* (1989); and the "coercion" test first used by the Court in *Lee*.

[2] In 1971, in the context of unconstitutional state aid to nonpublic schools, the Supreme Court in *Lemon* set forth the following test for evaluating alleged Establishment Clause violations. To survive the "*Lemon* test," the government conduct

in question (1) must have a secular purpose, (2) must have a principal or primary effect that neither advances nor inhibits religion, and (3) must not foster an excessive government entanglement with religion. The Supreme Court applied the *Lemon* test to every Establishment case it decided between 1971 and 1984, with the exception of *Marsh v. Chambers* (1983), the case upholding legislative prayer.

In the 1984 *Lynch* case, which upheld the inclusion of a nativity scene in a city's Christmas display, Justice O'Connor wrote a concurring opinion in order to suggest a "clarification" of Establishment Clause jurisprudence.

[3] Justice O'Connor's "endorsement" test effectively collapsed the first two prongs of the *Lemon* test:

> The Establishment Clause prohibits government from making adherence to a religion relevant in any way to a person's standing in the political community. Government can run afoul of that prohibition in two principal ways. One is excessive entanglement with religions institutions. . . . The second and more direct infringement is government endorsement or disapproval of religion. Endorsement sends a message to nonadherents that they are outsiders, not full members of the political community, and an accompanying message to adherents that they are insiders, favored members of the political community.

Religious Coercion

[4] The Court formulated the "coercion test" when it held unconstitutional the practice of including invocations and benedictions in the form of "nonsectarian" prayers at public school graduation ceremonies. Declining to reconsider the validity of the *Lemon* test, the Court in *Lee* found it unnecessary to apply the *Lemon* test to find the challenged practices unconstitutional. Rather, it relied on the principle that "at a minimum, the Constitution guarantees that government may not coerce anyone to support or participate in religion or its exercise, or

otherwise to act in a way which establishes a state religion or religious faith, or tends to do so." . . .

Finally, in its most recent school prayer case [*Santa Fe Independent School District v. Doe* (2000)], the Supreme Court applied the *Lemon* test, the endorsement test, and the coercion test to strike down a school district's policy of permitting student-led "invocation" before high school football games. Citing *Lee*, the Court held that "the delivery of a pregame prayer has the improper effect of coercing those present to participate in an act of religious worship." Applying the *Lemon* test, the Court found that the school district policy was facially unconstitutional because it did not have a secular purpose. The Court also used language associated with the endorsement test. ("[T]his policy was implemented with the purpose of endorsing school prayer."); ("Government efforts to endorse religion cannot evade constitutional reproach based solely on the remote possibility that those attempts may fail.").

[5] We are free to apply any or all of the three tests, and to invalidate any measure that fails any one of them. Because we conclude that the school district policy impermissibly coerces a religious act and accordingly hold the policy unconstitutional, we need not consider whether the policy fails the endorsement test or the *Lemon* test as well.

A Profession of a Religious Belief

[6] In the context of the Pledge, the statement that the United States is a nation "under God" is a profession of a religious belief, namely, a belief in monotheism. The recitation that ours is a nation "under God" is not a mere acknowledgment that many Americans believe in a deity. Nor is it merely descriptive of the undeniable historical significance of religion in the founding of the Republic. Rather, the phrase "one nation under God" in the context of the Pledge is normative. To recite the Pledge is not to describe the United States; instead, it is to swear allegiance to the values for which the flag stands:

unity, indivisibility, liberty, justice, and—since 1954—monotheism. A profession that we are a nation "under God" is identical, for Establishment Clause purposes, to a profession that we are a nation "under Jesus," a nation "under Vishnu," a nation "under Zeus," or a nation "under no god," because none of these professions can be neutral with respect to religion. The school district's practice of teacher-led recitation of the Pledge aims to inculcate in students a respect for the ideals set forth in the Pledge, including the religious values it incorporates.

The Supreme Court recognized the normative and ideological nature of the Pledge in [*West Virginia State Board of Education v. Barnette* (1943)]. There, the Court held unconstitutional a school district's wartime policy of punishing students who refused to recite the Pledge and salute the flag. The Court noted that the school district was compelling the students "to declare a belief" and "requir[ing] the individual to communicate by word and sign his acceptance of the political ideas [the flag] . . . bespeaks." "[T]he compulsory flag salute and pledge requires affirmation of a belief and an attitude of mind." The Court emphasized that the political concepts articulated in the Pledge were idealistic, not descriptive: "'[L]iberty and justice for all,' if it must be accepted as descriptive of the present order rather than an ideal, might to some seem an overstatement." The Court concluded that: "If there is any fixed star in our constitutional constellation, it is that no official, high or petty, can prescribe what shall be orthodox in politics, nationalism, religion, or other matters of opinion or force citizens to confess by word or act their faith therein."

A Coercive Policy

[7] The school district's policy here, like the school's action in *Lee,* places students in the untenable position of choosing between participating in an exercise with religious content or protesting. The defendants argue that the religious content of

"one nation under God" is minimal. To an atheist or a believer in non-Judeo-Christian religions or philosophies, however, this phrase may reasonably appear to be an attempt to enforce a "religious orthodoxy" of monotheism, and is therefore impermissible. As the Court observed with respect to the graduation prayer in *Lee:* "What to most believers may seem nothing more than a reasonable request that the nonbeliever respect their religious practices, in a school context may appear to the nonbeliever or dissenter to be an attempt to employ the machinery of the State to enforce a religious orthodoxy."

[8] The coercive effect of the policy here is particularly pronounced in the school setting given the age and impressionability of schoolchildren, and their understanding that they are required to adhere to the norms set by their school, their teacher and their fellow students. Furthermore, under *Lee,* non-compulsory participation is no basis for distinguishing *Barnette* from the case at bar because, even without a recitation requirement for each child, the mere presence in the classroom every day as peers recite the statement "one nation under God" has a coercive effect. The coercive effect of the Pledge is also made even more apparent when we consider the legislative history of the Act that introduced the phrase "under God." These words were designed to be recited daily in school classrooms. President Eisenhower, during the Act's signing ceremony, stated: "From this day forward, the millions of our school children will daily proclaim in every city and town, every village and rural schoolhouse, the dedication of our Nation and our people to the Almighty." All in all, there can be little doubt that under the controlling Supreme Court cases the school district's policy fails the coercion test.

The Supreme Court has addressed the Pledge in passing, and we owe due deference to its dicta. Our opinion, however, is not inconsistent with this dicta. In *Allegheny,* the Court noted that it had "considered in dicta the motto and the pledge, characterizing them as consistent with the proposition that government may not communicate an endorsement of religious belief." And in *Lynch,* the Court observed that students recited the pledge daily, but only to support its point that there is a long tradition of "official acknowledgment" of religion. Neither of these two references speaks to the issue here. We may assume *arguendo* [for the sake of argument] that public officials do not unconstitutionally endorse religion when they recite the Pledge, yet it does not follow that schools may coerce impressionable young schoolchildren to recite it, or even to stand mute while it is being recited by their classmates. . . .

A Violation of the Establishment Clause

[9] In light of Supreme Court precedent, we hold that the school district's policy and practice of teacher-led recitation of the Pledge, with the inclusion of the added words "under God," violates the Establishment Clause.

"Forcing Atheist children to hear [the Pledge of Allegiance] every day is nothing less than coercive brainwashing."

The Pledge of Allegiance Disenfranchises Atheist Students

Frank R. Zindler

In June 2002 the U.S. Court of Appeals for the Ninth Circuit ruled that teacher-led recitations of the Pledge of Allegiance, which includes the phrase "under God," violates the Establishment Clause of the First Amendment, which states, "Congress shall make no law respecting an establishment of religion." Two years later the Supreme Court reversed the decision because the man who had brought the case to the appellate court, Michael Newdow, lacked legal standing to sue his daughter's school district.

In the following viewpoint Frank R. Zindler condemns the Supreme Court's failure to uphold the Ninth Circuit Court's ruling that declared the Pledge of Allegiance unconstitutional. As a result of the Supreme Court's rules, he fears that atheist children will continue to be marginalized by the American government. Zindler contends that children who do not want to recite the pledge, in particular the phrase "under God," are viewed as un-American by their teachers and fellow students. He adds that being forced to hear the Pledge of Allegiance each day is a form of brainwashing. Zindler is the editor of American Atheist *magazine and the director of the American Atheist Press.*

The Supreme Court of the United States has ruled that Atheist Michael Newdow's brilliant victory over the prayer

Frank R. Zindler, "Prayer of Allegiance to Continue," *American Atheist,* Summer 2004.

of allegiance to the flag in a court of appeal is null and void—on the ground that he did not have standing to sue. This means that public school children all over the country will once again have to suffer the insult of "ceremonial deism" and endure the ritualized religious assaults of zealous authorities. Fortunately, the court did not rule on the merits of the case, and so it has not spoken one way or the other on the constitutionality of the prayer of allegiance. No precedent has been set . . . yet.

Atheists Are Unwelcome

It is not easy to be an Atheist in America, and it often is not pleasant. Everywhere we turn, we get the message "You are not wanted here."

In 'the year of our Lord' 1955, the motto "IN GOD WE TRUST" was inscribed on all the money we handle—even currency with the images of Infidels such as Abraham Lincoln, Thomas Jefferson, and Susan B. Anthony has been thus sanctified. The currency has effaced the free-thinking character of the persons honored. My own objection to the motto ended my twenty-year career as a teacher.

In 1956 the national motto "IN GOD WE TRUST" was adopted and trumpeted everywhere. There is a movement to plaster this patently false proposition above the porticoes of all public buildings and on the walls of every school room. Even before these two breaches were made in the wall of separation between state and church—in 1954—the pledge of allegiance to the flag of the United states had been altered so that today, when we are asked to pledge allegiance to the American flag, we are required either to say a prayer to a being we know to be imaginary, or risk being rejected as being un-American and un-patriotic.

When George Bush I was campaigning in Chicago for the presidency, American Atheist Press reporter Rob Sherman asked him what he would do for the Atheist population of our country. Bush's answer was difficult to understand, and Rob followed up with the question, "But surely, you are not questioning the patriotism or citizenship of Atheist Americans?"

Bush replied, "No, I don't think Atheists should be considered patriots or citizens—this is ONE NATION UNDER GOD." You may recognize that as a quote from the pledge.

The History of the Pledge

All three religious violations of America's secular constitution were committed during the Cold War of the '50s, and all three were intended to insult and disenfranchise Atheist Americans. Atheism was equated to Communism. Again and again, Atheist Americans were told to "Go back to Russia."

The history of how the pledge was changed shows there was a deliberate attempt to denigrate, marginalize, and disenfranchise Atheists.

The Knights of Columbus in New York City—archenemies of free thought, secular government, and the liberties guaranteed by the First Amendment—first added "under God" on April 22, 1951, and started a campaign to get all Knights of Columbus to do it. This was accomplished on August 21, 1952. Then they started a campaign to get the President and Congress to make it a law or at least a resolution. Then the American Legion picked up the religious fever. (Like the Boy Scouts, they still do not allow Atheists to be members.)

Supposedly, the words UNDER GOD were a quotation from Lincoln's Gettysburg Address. . . . Lincoln did not use those words. . . . It appears the words were added by Lincoln's secretary, who advised the unpopular president to appease his religious critics who were appalled by his lack of Christian beliefs.

As can be seen from the Congressional Record of the period, the Prayer of Allegiance was intended from the beginning to be an attack on Atheism and Atheists. Pres. Dwight D. Eisenhower, approving the sacralization of the pledge said:

> In this way we are reaffirming the transcendence of religious faith in America's heritage and future; in this way we shall constantly strengthen those spiritual weapons which forever will be our country's most powerful resource in peace and war.

In one sentence, Eisenhower denied the crucial importance of heretics in America's history. Where would we be without Ethan Allen, Thomas Paine, Thomas Jefferson, Ulysses S. Grant, and Abraham Lincoln?

Eisenhower also said,

> From this day forward, the millions of our school children will daily proclaim in every city and town, every village and rural schoolhouse, the dedication of our nation and our people to the Almighty—a patriotic oath AND A PUBLIC PRAYER. . . . Over the globe millions have been deadened in mind and soul by a materialistic philosophy of life.

Eisenhower did not care if among the millions coerced into prayer there might be Atheists. They were not Americans worth counting. Eisenhower got this idea from a sermon he had heard—the text of which was published in the *Congressional Record*, would you believe? The sermon was preached by George Docherty on 7 Feb 1954 and it galvanized the president and members of Congress to turn the pledge into a sacrament.

An Influential Sermon

According to Docherty,

> There was something missing in this pledge, and that which was missing was the characteristic and definitive facto in the American way of life. Indeed, apart from the mention of the phrase, the United States of America, this could be a pledge of any republic. In fact, I could hear the little Muscovites re-

peat a similar pledge to their hammer-and-sickle flag in Moscow with equal solemnity, for Russia is also a republic that claims to have over-thrown the tyranny of kingship.

In response to possible objections from Atheists, the minister declared "an atheistic American is a contradiction in terms." Pure atheists, according to Docherty, are little more than "spiritual parasites."

A more focused attack against Atheist Americans can scarcely be imagined, yet Docherty's words were repeated when the pledge resolution was taken up several days later in Congress. Said Rep. [Louis Charles] Rabaut, in restating his initial proposal, H.J. Res. 243,

> You may argue from dawn to dusk about differing political, economic, and social systems, but the fundamental issue which is the unbridgeable gap between America and Communist Russia is a belief in Almighty God. From the root of atheism stems the evil weed of communism and its branches of materialism and political dictatorship. Unless we are willing to affirm our belief in the existence of God and His creator-creature relation to man, we drop man himself to the significance of a grain of sand and open the floodgates to tyranny and oppression.

That is the same sort of reasoning that had caused seven states to include impediments to Atheists in their state constitutions. Three of these are still in force: Arkansas, Pennsylvania, and South Carolina.

Brainwashing Children

To appreciate how Atheists felt when all this was going on— and still feel as we continue to suffer the insult of attempted disenfranchisement—imagine how a Jew might feel if the pledge had been changed to read:

> I pledge allegiance to the flag, of the United States of America, and to the republic for which it stands, one nation, indivisible, with liberty and justice for Gentiles.

This would exclude Jews in exactly the same way that the current pledge excludes Atheists. The present pledge translates quite precisely into "with liberty and justice for believers," or "with liberty and justice for all except atheists." It should be noted that [Francis] Bellamy, the original author of the pledge, wanted to include "equality" along with liberty and justice, but he knew that would not fly. How could one imagine women and blacks on an equal basis with white men? To this day, "equality" has not made its way into the pledge—but an imaginary character has!

Forcing Atheist children to hear this litany every day is nothing less than coercive brainwashing. Children who don't say the pledge are viewed by teachers and students as "not one of us"—i.e., true Americans. This is an injury. It is frequently argued that adding "under God" to the pledge does not respect an establishment of religion. This flies in the face of the grammar that frames the wording of the First Amendment.

The intention of the writers of the First Amendment is clear from the grammar of its phrasing: "Congress shall make no law respecting an establishment of religion. . . ."

Please note the phrase does NOT read: "respecting an establishment of A religion. . . ."

The lack of the indefinite article shows the writers intended to prohibit not only the establishment of a particular sect, but intended to prohibit the elevation of religion in general above secular philosophies or non-religion. It is a pity that logic has no bearing upon such politically charged issues as the pledge question. To an Atheist it is self-evident that the flag cannot "stand" for something that does not exist. 'One nation under God' is a non-existent entity.

"Offering students the option to recite 'under God' along with their Pledge hardly reaches [the] level of religious establishment."

The Supreme Court Should Declare the Pledge of Allegiance Constitutional

Cheryl K. Chumley

Cheryl K. Chumley asserts in the following viewpoint that the Supreme Court erred by not ruling on the constitutionality of the Pledge of Allegiance when it overturned the Ninth Circuit Court's ruling that had declared the pledge unconstitutional. She opines that reciting the pledge, which contains the phrase "under God," cannot be considered religious indoctrination. Furthermore, Chumley maintains, students are not compelled to recite the Pledge of Allegiance. Therefore, recitation of the Pledge of Allegiance in public schools does not violate the First Amendment. Chumley is a contributing columnist to several Internet news services.

The Supreme Court justices may have dropped the ball on this one.

In 1954, at the height of concerns over the spread of communism, Congress voted to insert "under God" into our country's Pledge of Allegiance. In a nation of believers who by and large understand the Judeo-Christian principles involved with the founding of our constitutional system of governance, this hardly seemed inappropriate.

But self-professed atheist Michael Newdow disagreed, and so he did what most with a special interest axe to grind ultimately do—he sought redress in the courts.

Ducking the Issue

In 2002, the liberal 9th Circuit Court of Appeals ruled the "under God" phrase of the Pledge was unconstitutional. Public outcry ensued, especially after it was revealed Newdow seemingly and callously used his grade-school daughter, who never complained about the Pledge in the first place and was in fact being raised by a born-again Christian mother with full legal custody rights, to springboard his case into court.

The issue proceeded to the U.S. Supreme Court for clarification, and on Flag Day the ruling was made public. The result? Michael Newdow does not possess the legal standing, or authority, to bring this case before the court.

This decision is akin to a hard-charging, heart-pounding playoff game ending in a tie: In neither case can either side claim an uncontested win. And this is where the justices may have erred. By avoiding the merits of the case and ruling instead on a technicality, they have left the door open for further lawsuits and challenges questioning the constitutional aspects of the phrase "under God."

"The justices ducked this constitutional issue today, but it is certain to come back in the future," promised Rev. Barry Lynn, the executive director of Americans United for the Separation of Church and State.

Not Establishing a Religion

This piddling argument with anti-Christian organizations and individuals is becoming a bore.

Aside from the absolute ridiculousness of claiming simple utterance of the phrase "under God" is tantamount to religious indoctrination, as Newdow alleged, the entire argument groups like Lynn's use to advance their perceived notions of legal rights and wrongs is rooted in deception. The term "separation of church and state," the very terminology peddled by most anti-religious fanatics to keep all things Christian from the public domain, does not even exist in the Constitution.

What does exist, however, is the 1st Amendment and its mandate that "Congress shall make no law respecting an establishment of religion, or prohibiting the free exercise thereof," a clear-cut phrase that clear minds should interpret as an allowance for the people, rather than as a whip for the government to hold. What it means is Congress cannot, say, do as Iraq, which even with its new system of democracy declares itself a nation of Islam, bound by government law to uphold that religion's doctrines.

Offering students the option to recite "under God" along with their Pledge hardly reaches this level of religious establishment.

Had Newdow's daughter been forced by her teacher to say the phrase "under Jehovah," or "under Mohammed" or "under the Goddess of the Trees," perhaps he and his anti-Christian cohorts could have justifiably argued that the taxpayer-funded school system was attempting to establish and promote one form of religion over another.

Making a Choice

But that's not the case here, and neither was it found that this particular California public school, or any other for that matter, compels its students by means of physical force or emotional duress to say the Pledge or the "under God" phrase at all. Rather, the choice to participate in this act of patriotism is just that—a choice.

It's too bad the justices for the highest court in the land didn't exercise their choice, too, and issue forth a decisive ruling based on case merits with potential to end the debate over 1st Amendment rights once and for all. Instead, they granted the nation a reprieve—nothing more, nothing less—and displayed, in the process and in the words of Focus on the Family's Dr. James Dobson, "a lack of principle that is truly appalling."

> "The Pledge was/is basically a device to brainwash children from a very young age that their lives should be totally devoted to the State."

The Pledge of Allegiance Is a Form of Political Indoctrination

Bill Barnwell

Bill Barnwell argues in the following viewpoint that the debate over the words "under God" in the Pledge of Allegiance is beside the point. The pledge is offensive, but not because it can be seen as religious indoctrination. Rather, Barnwell argues, the Pledge of Allegiance is a political device that brainwashes students into becoming completely devoted to the state at the expense of their freedoms. Barnwell is a pastor in Swartz Creek, Michigan.

The real problem with the Pledge of Allegiance is not the phrase "under God." It's the whole concept of the pledge itself. While religious conservatives are rightfully outraged by judicial attempts to purge God from the public square, they should be cautious in their overall support for the Pledge, which is a tool of politicians to make our supreme loyalty the government.

Many people were rightfully taken aback [in 2002] when a western liberal appeals court struck down the phrase "under God" from the Pledge of Allegiance, saying it violated the "establishment clause" of the U.S. Constitution that "separates church and state." Only problem is the so-called "establishment clause" (When the framers wrote the constitution, they

Bill Barnwell, "I Pledge My Allegiance to the State," www.lewrockwell.com, June 19, 2004. Copyright © 2004 by LewRockwell.com. Reproduced by permission of the publisher and author.

had no idea that what they were writing included all these "clauses") was never intended to block saying nice things about God in public, it was designed to prevent the "establishment" of a state religion as was the case in Mother Britain before the Revolutionary War, where subjects were forced to belong to the Church of England. That was the whole purpose of the "establishment clause," but now liberals have gone wild in the post FDR [Franklin Delano Roosevelt] era with their blatant anti-Christian interpretations of law in their efforts to create a secular utopia.

Sidestepping the Issue

How saying "under God" in the Pledge establishes Christianity or anything else as a State Religion is beyond me, but our black-robed masters on the bench know better than the rest of us I suppose.

The guy that brought the case was Michael Newdow, an obvious anti-Christian crank. He brought it on behalf of his daughter (who along with her mother has no problem with the pledge) saying that the pledge was indoctrinating. A federal appeals court overturned a previous ruling from a lower court and struck down "under God" from the pledge. It was challenged and went to the Supreme Court. Many of us watched with curiosity for months as the case went before the Court and we waited for their opinion. Then [in June 2004] they wussed out just like many of us thought.

The Supremes overturned the earlier ruling that struck down "under God." But not because they felt the appeals court used screwy constitutional reasoning, but because Newdow didn't have the right to bring the suit on his daughter's behalf since he did not have full legal custody. Basically, the case was dismissed on a technicality and as such there is nothing from preventing this whole thing from starting all over again. The Supremes sidestepped the larger constitutional issues, as they often do, and really no one should be totally happy about this, including Pledge enthusiasts.

It's true that Newdow was acting like a dipstick by bringing this suit, using his daughter as a vehicle to push his anti-religious agenda. But if anything the reasoning of the Court helps to further solidify anti-father bias in judicial reasoning. If the Court's reasoning is taken to its logical conclusions then a father like Newdow has few if any rights over his daughter (even though he has visitation rights part of the month). The unfair bias towards mothers in custody cases and divorce proceedings is another topic for another time though.

The Pledge Is a Political Tool

Now let me get back to my main reason for writing this. I have no problem with the words "under God" being included in the Pledge of Allegiance. I love God and spend most my time serving Him. My problem is with the whole concept of the Pledge itself. The Pledge was/is basically a device to brainwash children from a very young age that their lives should be totally devoted to the State. The daily ritual in public schools of making little boys and girls stand up, put their hands over their hearts and "pledge their allegiance" to Uncle Sam is something very fitting for our Post-Lincoln nation, which ceased to be a Republic a long time ago and is now a continually growing statist empire that seeks to train children as early as possible to understand that their lives are not their own, and not even primarily God's, but the government's.

The phrase "under God" wasn't even added until 1954, in an attempt to basically, as [prominent libertarian] Lew Rockwell has said, "deify the State." It was added by Eisenhower and his Congress as a political tool during the Cold War to fight the "godless Communists" (as if the US has been the pristine example of being Godly). "Under God," therefore, was basically a political tool, used in a political war, by political people, to exert more political control over the masses.

In a system which people face a mandatory confiscation of 1/3 or more of their earned income a year, where federal, state and local laws criminalize almost everything under the sun, where regulations hamper one's ability to run a business or live a free life in the economic realm, where practicing and living out one's faith makes them susceptible for persecution, and where the lives of young people can be drafted to fight at a whim in wars they do not want or support to die for some political cause, the message is loud and clear: Your life is not your own, and not even God's, it belongs to the State.

The Pledge is a seemingly innocent tool to help get that point across under the guise of "patriotism." While we should of course punish those who engage in treason (by the way, treason is more than criticizing public officials or public policy, contrary to what authoritarians like Ann Coulter and even some religious conservatives think), and support love of country, the whole concept of a "Pledge of Allegiance" to the government is troublesome.

Political Indoctrination

The real scandal of the Pledge is not the phrase "under God," it's the whole Pledge itself and the concept behind it. The criticism of "under God" is a slap in the face to religious people, mainly Christians; but the real problem is not church-going people who worship the Lord, it is statists who worship the government. Yes, there is some indoctrinating going on with the Pledge, but the indoctrination is not religious, it is political and statist. It's high time for Christians to tell our rulers and masters in Washington, D.C., that our allegiance is to Christ, and not to them.

Organizations to Contact

American Civil Liberties Union (ACLU)
125 Broad St., Eighteenth Fl., New York, NY   10004-2400
(212) 549-2500
e-mail: aclu@aclu.org • Web site: www.aclu.org

The ACLU is a national organization that works to defend Americans' civil rights guaranteed by the U.S. Constitution. The Web site includes a section on students' rights, with information on topics such as freedom of expression, right to privacy, drug tests, and freedom of religion. The ACLU offers policy statements, pamphlets, its *Student Organizing Manual*, and the semiannual newsletter *Civil Liberties Alert.*

American Library Association (ALA)
50 E. Huron St., Chicago, IL   60611
(800) 545-2433
e-mail: library@ala.org • Web site: www.ala.org

The ALA supports intellectual freedom and private and free access to library materials. ALA's sister organization, the Freedom to Read Foundation, provides legal defense in important First Amendment cases involving libraries' rights to acquire and make available materials representing all points of view. The ALA publishes the *Newsletter on Intellectual Freedom*, pamphlets, articles, and posters. It also distributes the Banned Books Week Resource Kit.

Americans United for Separation of Church and State (AUSCS)
518 C St. NE, Washington, DC   20002
(202) 466-3234 • fax: (202) 466-2587
e-mail: americansunited@au.org • Web site: www.au.org

Through litigation, education, and advocacy, AUSCS works to protect religious freedom for all Americans. It opposes the passing of federal or state laws that threaten the separation of church and state and believes that parents, not schools, have the right to determine their children's exposure to religion. It prints brochures such as *Prayer and the Public Schools* and *Religion, Education, and Your Rights,* pamphlets, and the monthly newsletter *Church and State.*

Concerned Women for America (CWA)
1015 Fifteenth St. NW, Suite 1100
  Washington, DC   20005
(202) 488-7000 • fax: (202) 488-0806
e-mail: mail@cwfa.org • Web site: www.cwfa.org

CWA's purpose is to preserve, protect, and promote traditional Judeo-Christian values through education, legislative action, and other activities. It is concerned with creating an environment that is conducive to building strong families and raising healthy children. Publications relating to students' rights include *School Prayer and Religious Liberty: A Constitutional Perspective,* along with many articles in their monthly magazine *Family Voice.*

Drug Policy Alliance
70 West Thirty-Sixth St., Sixteenth Floor
  New York, NY   10018
(212) 613-8020 • fax: (212) 613-8021
e-mail: nyc@drugpolicy.org • Web site: www.drugpolicy.org

The Drug Policy Alliance is dedicated to studying alternatives to the war on drugs. One section of its Web site focuses on the issue of drug testing students, which the alliance opposes. The organization, which has headquarters in several cities throughout the United States, supports legalization of drug use, though not for minors, as well as the repeal of the drug provision of the Higher Education Act. Publications available on the Web site include the quarterly *Drug Policy Letter* and the paper *Drug Testing in Schools: Policies, Practices, and Association with Student Drug Use.*

Freechild Project

PO Box 6185, Olympia, WA   98507
(360) 753-2686
e-mail: info@freechild.org • Web site: www.freechild.org

The Freechild Project is a think tank, resource agency, and advocacy group for young people around the world who seek to play a larger role in their schools and communities. Training and conferences are offered to help parents, teachers, and community leaders involve youth in their communities. The Freechild Project's students' rights directory, which offers a wealth of information about school uniforms, zero tolerance, free speech, and student equality, can be accessed on the Web site, along with booklets, fact sheets, speeches, and book reviews.

Institute for Urban and Minority Education

Teachers College, Columbia University,
   Theresa Towers, Eighth Floor, 2090 Adam
   Clayton Powell Jr. Blvd., New York, NY   10027
(212) 678-3780 • fax: (212) 678-4137
Web site: iume.tc.columbia.edu

The institute conducts research and provides information on issues relating to educational opportunity, multiculturalism, and the reforms needed to improve the achievement of minority students. Its Web site also features an archive of material developed by the now-defunct ERIC Clearinghouse on Urban Education, including reports on drug testing and school violence.

National Coalition Against Censorship (NCAC)

275 Seventh Ave., New York, NY   10001
(212) 807-6222 • fax: (212) 807-6245
e-mail: ncac@ncac.org • Web site: www.ncac.org

NCAC is an alliance of organizations committed to defending freedom of thought, inquiry, and expression by engaging in public education and advocacy on national and local levels. Its

Web site contains a section on student rights. NCAC publishes booklets, such as *Public Education, Democracy, Free Speech: The Ideas That Define and Unite Us,* periodic reports, and the quarterly *Censorship News.*

National Education Association (NEA)
1201 Sixteenth St. NW, Washington, DC   20036
(202) 833-4000 • fax: (202) 822-7974
Web site: www.nea.org

NEA is America's oldest and largest volunteer-based organization dedicated to advancing the cause of public education. Its commitments at the local, state, and national levels include conducting workshops for teachers, lobbying for needed school resources and higher educational standards, and spearheading innovative projects that reshape the learning process. Two of NEA's publications, the monthly magazine *NEA Today Online* and biannual report *Thoughts and Action,* are available on its Web site. Issues such as drug testing, school safety, and religion in schools are also covered in their publications.

Office of National Drug Control Policy (ONDCP)
Drug Policy Information Clearinghouse,
   PO Box 6000, Rockville, MD   20849-6000
(800) 666-3332 • fax: (301) 519-5212
e-mail: ondcp@ncjrs.org • Web site: www.whitehousedrugpolicy.gov

The Office of National Drug Control Policy formulates the government's national drug strategy and the president's antidrug policy. Its goals are to reduce illicit drug use, manufacturing, and trafficking, drug-related crime and violence, and drug-related health consequences. Its reports include "What You Need to Know About Drug Testing in Schools" and "The Challenge in Higher Education: Confronting and Reducing Substance Abuse on Campus."

People for the American Way (PFAW)
2000 M St. NW, Suite 400, Washington, DC   20036

(202) 467-4999
e-mail: pfaw@pfaw.org • Web site: www.pfaw.org

PFAW is committed to reaffirming the traditional American values of pluralism, diversity, and freedom of expression and religion in many areas, including education. It is engaged in a mass media campaign to create a climate of tolerance and respect for diverse people, religions, and values. PFAW distributes educational materials, leaflets, and brochures and publishes the annual *Attacks on the Freedom to Learn*. Their Web site also addresses issues such as the privacy rights of students and religion in public schools.

Reason Foundation
3415 S. Sepulveda Blvd., Suite 400, Los Angeles, CA   90034
(310) 391-2245 • fax: (310) 391-4395
e-mail: gpassantino@reason.org • Web site: www.reason.org

This public policy organization researches contemporary social and political problems and promotes libertarian philosophy and free-market principles. It publishes the monthly *Reason* magazine, which contains articles and editorials on school drug policies and other education issues.

Student Press Law Center
1815 N. Fort Meyer Dr., Suite 900, Arlington, VA   22209
(703) 807-1904 • Web site: www.splc.org

An advocate for student free-press rights, the SPLC provides information, advice, and legal assistance to students and educators in their struggle to discuss important issues free from censorship. It operates a formal Attorney Referral Network of approximately 150 lawyers across the country that are available to provide free legal representation to students. The *SPLC Report* is printed three times a year.

For Further Research

Books

Kirk A. Bailey and Catherine J. Ross, *School Safety and Youth Violence: A Legal Primer.* Washington, DC: George Washington University, 2001.

William C. Bosher Jr., Kate R. Kaminski, and Richard S. Vacca, *The School Law Handbook: What Every Leader Needs to Know.* Alexandria, VA: Association for Supervision and Curriculum Development, 2004.

Haig A. Bosmajian, ed., *The Freedom to Publish.* New York: Neal-Schuman, 1989.

Barbara Flicker, ed., *Justice and School Systems: The Role of the Courts in Education Litigation.* Philadelphia: Temple University Press, 1990.

James W. Fraser, *Between Church and State: Religion and Public Education in a Multicultural America.* New York: St. Martin's Press, 1999.

Robert M. Hardaway, *America Goes to School: Law, Reform, and Crisis in Public Education.* Westport, CT: Praeger, 1995.

Charles Haynes et al., *The First Amendment in Schools.* Alexandria, VA: Association for Supervision and Curriculum Development, 2003.

Patricia H. Hinchey, *Student Rights: A Reference Handbook.* Santa Barbara: ABC-CLIO, 2001.

John C. Hogan, *The Schools, the Courts, and the Public Interest.* Lexington, MA: Lexington Books, 1985.

David L. Hudson Jr., *The Silencing of Student Voices: Preserving Free Speech in American Schools.* Nashville: First Amendment Center, 2004.

Peter Irons, ed., *May It Please the Court: Courts, Kids, and the Constitution.* New York: New Press, 2000.

John W. Johnson, *The Struggle for Student Rights:* Tinker vs. Des Moines *and the 1960s.* Lawrence: University Press of Kansas, 1997.

Michael W. LaMorte, *School Law: Cases and Concepts.* Englewood Cliffs, NJ: Prentice-Hall, 1992.

Robert Wheeler Lane, *Beyond the Schoolhouse Gate: Free Speech and the Inculcation of Values.* Philadelphia: Temple University Press, 1995.

Office of National Drug Control Policy, *What You Need to Know About Drug Testing in Schools.* Washington, DC: Office of National Drug Control Policy, September 20, 2002.

Ellen Frankel Paul, *The Right to Privacy.* New York: Cambridge University Press, 2000.

People for the American Way, *A Right-Wing and a Prayer: The Religious Right and Your Public Schools.* Washington, DC: People for the American Way, 1997.

Jamin B. Raskin, *We the Students: Supreme Court Decisions for and About Students.* Washington, DC: CQ Press, 2003.

Kevin W. Saunders, *Saving Our Children from the First Amendment.* New York: New York University Press, 2003.

Traci Truly, *Teen Rights: A Legal Guide for Teens and the Adults in Their Lives.* Naperville, IL: Sphinx, 2002.

Periodicals

America, "Dictates of Common Sense," February 9, 1985.

American Civil Liberties Union, "Your Right to Privacy," www.aclu.org.

Richard Glen Boire, "Dangerous Lessons," *Humanist,* November/December 2002.

Erwin Chemerinksy, "One Nation Under the Constitution," *Church & State,* December 2003.

Christian Century, "Taking on the Pledge," July 17, 2002.

Barbara Dority, "Big Brother Goes to High School," *Humanist,* March/April 1997.

Donald A. Dripps, "Will the Real Fourth Amendment Please Stand Up?" *Trial,* November 1995.

Kathy Dunn and Steven King, "Should Students Have to Take Drug Tests to Participate in Extracurricular Activities?" *NEA Today,* January 2005.

Richard W. Garnett, "Keep It to Yourself," *Commonweal,* August 13, 2004.

David L. Hudson Jr., "Underground Papers and Off-Campus Speech," First Amendment Center, www.firstamendment center.org.

Wendy Kaminer, "Religion, Public Schools, and Gray Areas," *Free Inquiry,* April/May 2001.

———, "The War on High Schools," *American Prospect,* December 20, 1999.

Jack Keller, "School Searches," New York State Police, School, and Community Outreach Unit, May 20, 2003. www.cnypolice.com.

Dave Kindred, "Constitutional Rights—and Wrongs," *Sporting News,* July 10, 1995.

Kathleen Klink, "Freeing the Student Press for Their Good and Ours," *School Administrator,* April 2002.

Joseph R. McKinney, "The Effectiveness and Legality of Random Drug Testing Policies," www.studentdrugtest ing.org.

New York Times, "Unwarranted Student Drug Testing," June 28, 1995.

Michael Newdow, "Pledging Allegiance to My Daughter," *New York Times,* June 21, 2004.

Nathan Roberts, "Random Drug Testing of Students," *Journal of Law and Education,* April 2002.

Marsha Rosenbaum, "Random Student Drug Testing Is No Panacea," *Alcoholism & Drug Abuse Weekly,* April 12, 2004.

Herman Schwartz, "The Court's Terrible Two," *Nation,* July 22, 2002.

Jacob Sullum, "Let the Love Flow: Student Drug Testing," *Reason,* May 2004.

Abigail Thernstrom, "Courting Disorder in the Schools," *Public Interest,* Summer 1999.

David A. Toy, "The Pledge: The Constitutionality of an American Icon," *Journal of Law and Education,* January 2005.

Woody West, "High Court Should Pledge to Take a Stand," *Insight on the News,* April 27, 2004.

Jonathan Yardley, "High School Sense and Censorship," *Washington Post,* January 18, 1988.

Mark G. Yudof, "Principal as Publisher, Not Censor," *Wall Street Journal,* January 20, 1988.

Cathy Young, "One Nation, Many Gods," *Reason,* October 2002.

Perry A. Zirkel, "Courtside—the Games, They Are A-Changin,'" *Phi Delta Kappan,* October 2000.

———, "Drug Test Passes Court Test," *Phi Delta Kappan,* October 1995.

Web Sites

First Amendment Center Online (www.firstamendmentcen ter.org). This site features research, reports, and analysis on First Amendment topics, as well as an online library and news on free-expression issues. It is operated by the First Amendment Center, which has offices in Arlington, Virginia, and at Vanderbilt University in Nashville, Tennessee.

Privacy Watch—Student Rights (www.cotse.net/privacy/stu dent_rights.htm). This page is part of a Web site that lists dozens of links to issues relating to the right to privacy; it provides the latest news on student privacy and rights.

Index